Also by Gary Joseph Grappo

START YOUR OWN BUSINESS IN THIRTY DAYS
THE TOP 10 CAREER STRATEGIES FOR THE YEAR 2000 & BEYOND
THE TOP 10 FEARS OF JOB SEEKERS
GET THE JOB YOU WANT IN THIRTY DAYS

Career *ReExplosion*

Reinvent Yourself
in Thirty Days

GARY JOSEPH GRAPPO

BERKLEY BOOKS, NEW YORK

This book is an original publication of The Berkley Publishing Group.

CAREER REEXPLOSION

A Berkley Book / published by arrangement with the author

PRINTING HISTORY
Berkley trade paperback / July 2000

The Penguin Putnam Inc. World Wide Web site address is
http://www.penguinputnam.com

ISBN: 0-425-17444-1

BERKLEY®
Berkley Books are published by The Berkley Publishing Group,
a division of Penguin Putnam Inc.,
375 Hudson Street, New York, New York 10014.
BERKLEY and the "B" design
are trademarks belonging to Penguin Putnam Inc.

PRINTED IN THE UNITED STATES OF AMERICA

10 9 8 7 6 5 4 3 2 1

For Lucas and Erin

Contents

Introduction   1

ONE
My First Time   5

TWO
The Barriers   11

THREE
Return to Your Dreams   41

FOUR
Set the Stage   59

FIVE
Build a Bridge   77

SIX
Live the Dream Now   93

SEVEN
Take Action   109

EIGHT
Career ReExplosion Activity Planner   123

Bibliography   137
Contact the Author Directly   141

Charts and Exercises

Top Ten Career ReExplosion Warning Signs	3
Blast from the Past Quiz	13
Traditions	21
Individuals of Influence	23
Decision-Making Style Test	26
ILC Prescription for Longevity	31
My Personal Barriers to Career ReExplosion	37
Sample Childhood Interests List	43
Childhood Dreams and Interests Exercise	44
Current Dreams and Interests Exercise	47
Top Ten Dream Careers Exercise	49
Top Three Career ReExplosion Options	51
Steps to Balancing Career Goals and Family	55
Transferable Skills Inventory	62
Benefits to Having Mentors and Role Models	66
Do-Your-Research Tips	67
Ways to Volunteer	70
Benefits to Volunteering	71
Examples of Nonspecific and Nonactive Plans	79
Power List of Specific and Active Plans	80
Why Do You Need to Write a Plan?	83

Your Plan's Introduction 84

Questions to Ask Yourself About Fear 91

The Personal Time Survey 96

The Top Fears of Involving Others 101

Top Mistakes People Make in Promoting Themselves 104

Surround Yourself with Positive People Exercise 116

Health, Energy, and Fitness Review 117

Brittany, Delval, and Calby from Mrs. Elder's
Second Grade Class List of People Who Continued
Despite Difficulties 119

Mrs. Nelson's First Grade Class Quotes from
People Who Never Gave Up 119

Testimonials from Mrs. Nelson's First Grade Class 120

Tips to Have an Adult Attitude About Never Giving Up 121

Career ReExplosion

Introduction

"EMPLOYEES are surfing the Internet at work, calling in sick when they really feel fine and abandoning successful careers to go back to school," says Stephanie Armour in her *USA Today* article, "Boredom Drains Workers, Workforce" (May 21, 1999). Blaming much of job burnout on boredom is the premise of her story.

Nearly 45 percent of hiring experts say their firm lost top workers in 1998 because the company was unable to provide them with challenging growth opportunities, based on a recent survey by Exec-U-Net, a Norwalk, Connecticut–based networking organization for senior executives.

"A lot of people are in jobs they find boring or repetitive, and they feel trapped," says Beverly Potter, author of *Overcoming Job Burnout*. "Boredom is when your capabilities are greater than the task you are doing. It's actually stressful."

What is the fuel behind this national boredom and further fueling a massive desire for what I call Career ReExplosion? Several trends are detonating a bomb that has been waiting to happen:

- **Baby Boomers**
  Many have already put more than twenty years into a job. Many are not looking forward to a continued pattern of a lack of job stimulation and challenge. "It's doing the same darned thing too long," says author Peter Drucker.

- **Repetitive Service Jobs**
  Service jobs have become the repetitive-type factory jobs of the 2000s. The number of service jobs rose from about 82 million in 1989 to 102 million in March 1999, according to the U.S. Department of Labor. In the past, many manual labor–type jobs had continuous demands on workers, and they created burnout. Currently, the same scenario is now being replayed not in manufacturing but in the service industry. Many find themselves wanting out.

- **The Downsizing of American Businesses**
  In many cases, employees are working longer hours, doing more tasks, and even eating lunch at their desks in order to meet the demands of companies who had major layoffs in the '90s. Many experts agree that this factor alone has become a major force in stressing workers and propelling them to pursue dream careers, even when they discover the money may be less than what they currently are making.

With all that said, here are my top ten warning signs that you are in need of a Career ReExplosion. Circle the ones that apply to you.

TOP TEN CAREER REEXPLOSION WARNING SIGNS

1. A constant feeling of anger toward bosses and/or coworkers

2. Feeling helpless at work and more like a victim than a champion

3. A daily sense of being overwhelmed and never getting it all done

4. Not being given and/or not taking any new, creative, and challenging responsibilities

5. A constant sense of physical fatigue that never seems to go away

6. Maintaining a lazy attitude of "Don't mistake me for someone who cares."

7. Withdrawing from people more and more in your personal and professional life

8. Increased use of alcohol or the use of drugs

9. Surfing the Internet when you should be working

10. Calling in sick when you're really not

If you circled more than one of the above, you need a change. You can do it by reading on.

CHAPTER 1

My First Time

ALTHOUGH I did not know it at the time, I had my first experience with Career ReExplosion when I was in my late twenties. The idea of becoming someone completely new at an early stage in my life and career was out of the ordinary for me. After all, I was a theology major just a few years out of college. We weren't supposed to think that way. But there I was, fresh out of college, and I already had a restlessness and fascination for personal reinvention. I had thought about it many times but did not believe that it was even possible.

In school, I completed studies in theology at both the undergraduate and graduate levels. In my first years right out of college, the idea of pursuing a career in my field of study seemed like an unwanted possibility to me. I realized that in hindsight, the course work I had chosen was more about personal discovery than about planning for a career. But the course work, the money that I spent on it, and the resulting life I created had now overtaken me. I felt an obligation to my education.

At the peak of my frustration, I was twenty-eight. A major question went unanswered from almost the very day I graduated the master's program: Now that I've achieved this diploma, how can I move on from here and reinvent my life—my career? With the degrees I had, I felt trapped. There were other questions, too. Who would want an individual with two theology degrees and working on a third in law and ethics? Ideally, I really wanted to move my career to working in some aspect of the business world. How would I do it?

Near the end of my twenty-seventh year, I had a strange and repetitive dream. It became reflective of the reexplosion that was about to take place. In it, I was speaking to myself as well as to my friends a singular phrase that I repeated over and over—a mantra: "Free to be free, free to be me." Each time, upon waking from the dream, I was extremely optimistic. I believed I was free to become whatever it was that I wanted to be. I had an overwhelming sense that success was not just for the rich or a choice few. I had an enormous epiphany that the freedom of choice and success belonged to any person who desired it. Wow, what a freeing realization to come to at any age! Through the dream's message, I felt strengthened and encouraged that I could overcome all the barriers that were preventing me from reinventing myself.

The barriers! That's an understatement. There were many. Obviously, the big one was the self-imposed obligation I had to my education. Now, there's a good reason to remain unfulfilled in life. Another major one was spiritual. No matter how unhappy I was, it seemed certain that God wanted me to continue this career. Then there were my family and friends. I did not want to disappoint them and their perception of who I was and who I should remain. Additional considerations were that I lived in a conservative small town in Ohio while also owning a house, a new car, and a dog. All of it together added up to be an albatross of obstacles and barriers that had kept me up to this point from reinventing myself. There may have been more.

But back to that one repetitive and encouraging dream, the mantra: "Free to be free, free to be me." Did I believe it? Yes! Did I have my doubts? Yes! I realized that I had to overcome them. The only way to do it was to go out and begin to take small steps and do something about it.

One night after school, while attending doctoral classes in Pittsburgh, I called the YMCA looking for the most inexpensive room in the city. Once secure knowing that I had a $15 room for the night, I decided not to drive back home to Ohio after class. I planned to stay and do research in the library. Only this time it was not going to be researching obscure books on situational ethics. I made a commitment to myself to discover me. Secretly, I hoped that an evening of research and reflection would lead me to a breakthrough and shed light on a new life and career.

As I reclined on the library sofa, the *Pittsburgh Press* in my hand was reporting almost 12 percent unemployment for many of the cities in the region. I was looking for good news. This was definitely bad news and not what I had expected to find in my first hours of research. However, I did not let it deter me. Bad news and all, results were still achieved out of that one night's commitment to do something about my career.

Two weeks later, I was back at the same YMCA with another $15 room. I had recently been notified that I was one of many—approximately two thousand—who had responded to a *Pittsburgh Press* display ad and was selected for a prescreen interview. It was scheduled with interviewers from a new company in the New York area called People Express. It was for the position of customer service manager for an up-start low-cost airline.

Given the fact that I had no professional business experience and more importantly no airline experience, it seemed highly unlikely that I was going to get this job. Being one of two thousand applicants at the Pittsburgh Hilton waiting in a line for more than two hours for an interview reinforced my thoughts of inadequacy. All I had going for me was the fact that I had an innate passion for aircraft and an industry that I had loved since childhood. The passion I brought that day was born out of childhood flying experiences that left a deep and lasting impression upon me. It showed.

Initially, while going through the interview process, my self-perception made it virtually impossible to let me imagine myself as anything but a theology major. However, innately I knew that I had to repackage my previous education and experience if I was going to win. I also knew that I had to aggressively translate them into common skills that an interviewer could relate to if I was going to succeed at reinventing myself.

No longer was it an inexpensive room at the YMCA. I was moving up. The Howard Johnson at Newark Airport was where I would soon learn the results of this unlikely metamorphosis. I discovered that indeed I did effectively bridge and translate my education and skills into a dream career. I was one of two candidates hired from that recruitment event.

Unbelievably, one night's commitment in a library set the wheels of personal reinvention in motion. Success had an opportunity to create itself. Within one month of my decision to change my life and career, I had completed most of my initial interviews. Within three months of that day of research in the library, I had successfully launched my first Career ReExplosion. Moreover, I was officially working for a company and at a job that I thoroughly enjoyed, and I had successfully transformed myself from a theology major into the world of business.

This was just the beginning of many more personal "explosions" to come. I had experienced the thrill of my first personal reinvention. I felt secure that in the future, when there was a need to do it again, there would be no delays and no stopping me. I now had the power to reinvent myself at will at any stage in my life. There is a great sense of inner freedom that comes with that. It is *real* job security. No boss, no company, no past was going to render me helpless again.

Presently, for a variety of reasons, millions of people are entering their thirties, forties, fifties, sixties, and even their seventies seeking a new life and career. This book is about how to discover your own personal life and Career ReExplosion. As long as you remain open to learning, imagination, creativity, doing, trying, and ultimately rebelling against the past, all you should need is this book as your guide for a new dream career filled with happiness, excitement, new opportunities, freedom, passion, money, and success. Come join me!

In chapter 2, you assess your own barriers to Career ReExplosion. Then, in chapters 3 through 7, you discover the actual steps to detonating your own personal "explosion" within thirty days.

As you embark, keep in mind that a desire for personal reinvention is not enough. Practically everyone wants to reinvent themselves in one way or another. My commitment to you is that you will be coached step-by-step into specific results-oriented actions. That's what this book is all about, creating personal results by the time you have completed reading it. It's action-packed! This will be more fun than any action movie you have ever attended. Are you ready?

CHAPTER 2

The Barriers

YOU may be very anxious to begin mapping out your Career ReExplosion strategy. That will begin in chapter 3. However, take a few moments now and focus on the barriers to Career ReExplosion. Acknowledge the potential barriers that you may have acquired over the years, create awareness of them, help eliminate the brick walls that hold you back, and overcome any obstacles to change.

In this chapter, the objective is to identify barriers whether they are perceived or real, address them, and move on. Now you are ready for the powerful Career ReExplosion forces of change that lie ahead over the next thirty days.

The Barriers

Through my seminars and one-on-one counseling experiences, the barriers suffocating Career ReExplosion seem to come back to five areas of concern. They are:

1. The past

2. The personal

3. Medical issues

4. Technological issues

5. Company problems

As you read this chapter, carefully keep a record of the barriers that apply to you. Write them down in the section provided on the last page of this chapter. By writing them down and acknowledging them, you are best prepared psychologically to overcome the obstacles that thus far have hindered you from executing successful personal reinvention.

The Past

The past is a powerful force and has a substantial influence upon all aspects of our lives. It can determine what foods we eat, the friends we choose, how we spend money, and even how we direct our careers. H. S. Sullivan and his work in psychoanalysis throughout the 1900s theorized about the influence the past has upon our lives.

Sullivan believes, psychologically, that the adult is simply a set of internal structures based almost entirely on the past. He states, "Out of early interactions, infants become aware of themselves as 'good me' or 'bad me,' and [influenced by nurture] determines either a 'good mother' or 'bad mother,' depending on how successfully contact is accomplished. The later acquisition of language facilitates consolidation of 'good' and 'bad' into more complete personifications of self and others during childhood. *The essential roots of self are traced very early to past interactions with people.* This paradigm also has its origins in the work of sociologists C. H. Cooley and G. H. Mead." (This article, which first appeared in *Contemporary Psychoanalysis*, Vol. 24, 1988, pp. 548–576 as "Sullivan's Contribution to Psychoanalysis," was edited and condensed by Steven Tublin, Ph.D.)

Most of us are unaware of the hidden past. It has created certain personal presuppositions about what you believe you can or can not do ("good" and "bad") with your life and career. Take the Blast from the Past Quiz and uncover the past influences that have gotten you to where you are today. Carefully answer each question thoroughly and honestly. Use additional paper to provide enough writing space to answer the questions completely.

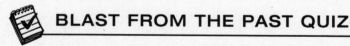

BLAST FROM THE PAST QUIZ

1. What is your earliest recollection about your parents' attitude toward working? What do you remember them saying about working? _____

_____

_____

_____

2. As you grew older, what did they say to you about getting a job and working? _____

_____

_____

_____

3. What was the message you heard from your teachers about choosing a career and preparing to enter the world of work?

_____

_____

_____

_____

4. How many jobs/careers did your father/mother have while you were growing up?

Father: _____

_____

Mother: _____

_____

5. How many jobs/careers did your grandfather and/or grand-mother have?

_____

_____

6. How do you feel the world of work has changed since the time period in which your father/mother worked?

_____

_____

_____

7. Do you believe that your father and mother each had the ideal job and career that they always wanted? Why or why not?

_____

_____

_____

8. When you try/tried to follow your dream career, how much encouragement do you or did you receive from your parents? What did they say to you about it? _____

_____

_____

_____

_____

_____

_____

9. Who made fun of what you wanted to do with your life besides possibly a parent? Was it a brother, sister, and/or friend? What did they say? _____

_____

_____

_____

_____

_____

10. Based on your past influences, what would you select if you could choose only one of the following? Circle one.

    a. Work at a job with less happiness but plenty of money.

    b. Work at a job with less money but plenty of happiness.

As can be imagined, many of your core values and perceptions about life and career have come from past influences. The bulk of the past influences, of course, were your mother, father, grandparents, siblings, teachers, and friends.

In these questions, what is possibly the number-one influence and message from the past still having an impact on you today? Probably it was your parents. If they are at all similar to mine, they were married to their jobs. They were one-career individuals. Probably your grandparents were the same.

Teachers and education have also promoted the one-career life. What can we recall about our schooling? Many have memories of beautifully illustrated career books where children played doctor, fireman, policeman, and nurse. The subtle message was that children are to grow up, choose a career, and as an adult be that person for the rest of one's life. Our parents' example in most cases reinforced this perception.

When did you get creative and want to try something new as a child or teenager? How did your parents respond? When I was twelve, I remember one incident in particular. It happened one day after school. "Dad, Mom," I said, "I want to learn how to play guitar." Immediately, a significant argument ensued. Many can relate, I'm sure. "You'll never practice," they said firmly. "If we know you, it will be a lot of wasted time and money for nothing." *Well, so much for trying something new*, I thought. Their unpleasant reaction and negative confrontation was one of many that sent a bad message about being inquisitive, creative, innovative, and desiring change. I discovered at a very early age not to outwardly express or entertain change, and from their reaction, not to rock the boat if I valued my own personal peace and harmony.

Whenever you tried to think creatively or tried to do something new, who were your critics? Was it only your parents? In my case, it was also a brother whose sole mission in life was to make my life miserable. He was highly negative and critical. Possibly, in your case, it may have been a brother, sister, or a friend. Peers are often highly critical of others because it is not respected or expected that one should rise above them and demonstrate success. Many peers who would actually encourage you to be creative and have multiple interests would be individuals admitting to personal failure. Most peer pressure dictates that if there are going to be any losers in the crowd, everyone in the group is going to lose together.

By the way, how did you answer question number ten? If you're like many, you selected number one. The message has been ingrained in us from birth: making money and paying the bills is what life is all about. Generally speaking, parents and the educational system place very little emphasis on what career author Marsha Sinetar counsels in her book *Do What You Love and the Money Will Follow*. Through my seminars and public speaking, I meet many individuals—engineers, doctors, lawyers, and many others—that as early as their late twenties and early thirties realize they have made a big investment in their careers and a big mistake. Many repeatedly say the same thing: "I do what I do because my parents and I thought that for the long term this would be the best income and job security for my life. Now I hate going to work, and I don't know what else I can do."

Although the past may dictate how we got to where we are today, it does not have to have an eternal grip. One thing we do know for certain: Past values and perceptions about work ingrained in us from birth are not working anymore. Let's take a look at other barriers to Career ReExplosion before embarking upon solutions and actions.

The Personal

Because the past is powerful, it creates the perception that even the personal hindrances to change—the ones you are responsible for—may be blamed on external forces beyond your control. Essentially, one could say, "I'm a victim; poor me." At first look, this removes the burden of taking personal responsibility for your present condition. But does it really?

In actuality, there are many personal barriers to change that you must take responsibility for if you are going to realize your dream career. In fact, if you had to select a barrier, this is probably the one you would want to choose the most. Personal issues are the ones that you have the most power to change. The personal barriers in this section range from your education and traditions to personal relationships and decision-making style.

Education

Education can be simultaneously a personal barrier and an asset. On the Internet, there is a frustrated midlife career changer visiting a forum that states it quite well. She writes, "I visited your forum for midlife career changers. I am trying to leave research science. I have been job searching in Chicago, totally without success, for a whole year despite having a Ph.D., being a published author, and having won awards as a clothing designer. You would think I've proven my versatility and ability to learn. I am now cashing in one of my retirement accounts to leave for Los Angeles, where I hope my chances will be better. But I'm wondering what is wrong with this country that it is so hard for a person to get a second start." In this case, education is a barrier when degrees are perceived as synonymous with the ticket to success. As soon to be discussed in chapter 4, reinvention takes more than being educated.

On one side of the coin, too much education may be perceived as a barrier because a person's life becomes very focused and their trained skill sets may appear to have limited use outside of their field. An example of this would be individuals who have studied law and discover at some point in their careers that they no longer wish to be lawyers. On the flip side of the coin, others may see too little education as a hindrance. Typically, these individuals conclude that they will have to put off their goals for reinvention until they become more educated.

As you can see, the education barrier rears its ugly head in a variety of ways. All of them seem valid to the person who believes it. In reality, whether it's too much or too little education, they all can't be right. As you will discover soon, it's how you attack Career ReExplosion with active steps that determines your success. Too much or too little education has nothing to do with successfully masterminding your own reinvention.

Tradition

Tradition is one of the central themes of *Fiddler on the Roof*, a major film and Broadway musical. "Where would we be without tradition?" states one of the classic lines from the production. The song "Tradition" soon follows. The conclusion of its central theme is that we don't really know why it is we do what we do. We simply do it—"well—because it's tradition!"

It is my personal belief that one of the major barriers to career

19

change lies solely in an individual's entrenchment in tradition. Don't get me wrong, some traditions are good. However, some are major obstacles when they prevent us from achieving our goals and do not let us escape dead-end jobs and lifestyles.

In my life, when People Express airlines began to suffer financially, I was forced into another Career ReExplosion. I decided to go into computer sales. The Southeast regional manager of Harris Corporation said that he hired me because I had the sense to leave my hometown in Ohio. As I stated earlier, it was an area with 12 percent unemployment. Little did I realize that my willingness to break away from the tradition of living in my hometown would become a future employer's leading indicator of my success. The regional hiring manager took notice of it in the interview and gave me yet another opportunity to reinvent myself by offering me a career in sales.

In brief, what traditions might be holding you back? For instance, are you young, single, and focusing all your energy on dating instead of taking steps and risks to blossom in the dream career you deserve? Are you stuck in a traditional mind-set that says if you're not married by the time you're twenty-five, thirty, or forty—whatever the age may be—you're over the hill? How about the limitations perpetrated by family and the resulting social expectations that say you're not successful unless you have the white picket fence, 2.5 children, and a three-car garage?

A friend in France recently gave up career explosion opportunities at an extremely young age by caving in to tradition. In her culture, if a daughter is not engaged by the age of twenty-four, a traditional French family will throw a party on the last day of October (feast of Saint Catharine) of the daughter's twenty-fourth year. At the party, the daughter is to wear a funny hat and be the focus of public jest. With all the extensive life and career opportunities she had going for her, tradition cut them short. She gave in and became engaged before October of her twenty-fourth year. She confided to me that she did not want to go through the thirtieth-of-October fiasco. Now that she will be married soon, the family's goals are that she should just maintain her current career, place any career growth on hold, have children, and probably withdraw completely from the workforce at some point within the next few years. As of a few months ago, she indicated that being the youngest of four children, it is imperative that she does not let the family down and must go through with the marriage. She feels obligated to this path not necessarily for herself but to fulfill traditional family expectations.

Some traditions are not as obvious as the one just described. Some are subtle and yet remain very powerful in their ability to prevent you from achieving your reinvention goals. How might the following list of traditions be influencing your inability to break through your barriers to change? Circle or list on a separate sheet of paper the ones that apply to you.

 ## TRADITIONS

- Attachment to a particular home or apartment

- Established relationships with a select group of coworkers or social friends

- Long-time familiarity with a particular job and task

- Achieved status in your community and/or job

- Ability to work close to home

- Attachment to the same daily work schedule

- Exceptional love of being the martyr, being unhappy, and the attention you get for it

- Unrealistic religious values that focus on miracles for success rather than taking action and hard work

- Attachment to your education and work history making you one-dimensional

- Established income level that says that is all you'll ever be worth

- A spouse who is attached to much of the above while you're not

Personal Relationships

The same relationships that bring happiness to your life can also be the source of some of the obstacles that keep you from reinventing yourself. In her book, *Successful Recareering*, Joyce Schwartz states, "WARNING: The advice of family and friends may be hazardous to your happiness." How true! Simple things that loved ones say and do all have a profound influence on what you are willing and not willing to do with your life. Of course, keep in mind that in many cases their stifling comments and behavior are not always intentional. At times, their negative comments may be out of ignorance, driven by their own upbringing, competitiveness, money issues, or the fear of being left behind in their career, just to mention a few.

Answer the following questions. Recall within the past five years when loved ones in your life have been critical of you and of any new goals and aspirations that you have had. When they were critical, how did that make you feel? More importantly, recall how much energy you have expended trying to convince someone close to you that your new ideas and direction are valid and worth pursuing. Who were they? Here is a partial list of individuals of influence you should monitor. Keep in mind that the words they speak and the actions they take have substantial power over your success.

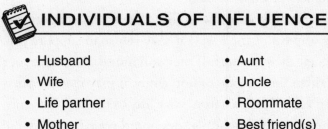

INDIVIDUALS OF INFLUENCE

- Husband
- Wife
- Life partner
- Mother
- Father
- Brother
- Sister
- Fiancée/fiancé
- Boyfriend
- Girlfriend

- Aunt
- Uncle
- Roommate
- Best friend(s)
- Teacher
- Boss
- Coworker
- Clergy
- Counselor

A natural reaction to this list is to think that to honor such important and respected people in your life is to follow their every word. Not true! If they truly love you, they will offer valuable feedback when necessary but relinquish all decision making to you and respect you for it. Unfortunately, this is not always the case. When their comments come across no longer as feedback but as demands, it's time to tune them out and realize that you are in charge. When it comes to your life, the buck stops with you. Only the strong and resolute will stand up against popular opinion and do what is hard, difficult, and necessary. The sooner you make a firm stand for your beliefs, no matter how unpopular they are, the sooner you will maintain control of your life, career, and ultimately your success. When you decide to hang on to every word of the influencers, ultimately they will not be there when you fail as a result of implementing their opinions. If you bear all the responsibility, in the final analysis you should be free to make all final decisions and take personal responsibility for their outcomes.

You need to surround yourself with loved ones who support you even though your way is not their way. If they refuse to support you, talk to them and elicit their support. If they still refuse, minimize your relationship with them. In the case of nonfamily, it may mean permanently separating these individuals from your life. In the case of family, work with them and remain resolute in designing your future. Avoid arguments, change the subject, tune them out, and go do what is best for you. Make a commitment today to associate with only positive and influential people.

Decision-Making Style

Your decision-making style could be another barrier keeping you from personal reinvention. Some individuals make decisions rapidly, and for them this obviously is not an issue. Others are slow in their decision making and are practically immobilized when it comes time to make even day-to-day decisions.

Your decision-making style has been acquired through the years from a variety of factors. Not all of them are external. Goleman, in his book *Emotional Intelligence*, has gathered research to show that many of our "soft" functions, such as decision making, are in some part shaped by biological and genetic factors, not just environmental as once was thought. Beyond the biogenetics, the external forces that have shaped

24

your decision-making style are your parents, education, work experiences, and the bosses that have managed you.

An illustration of how work experiences and bosses can influence decision making is a company that I briefly consulted for, who has what they call "The Wall of Shame." On it they post letters, situation descriptions, customer comments, and other reports that document publicly when employees mess up at their jobs. Prior to this knowledge, I had walked around the organization and had the impression that many of the people were slow to make decisions. Once I uncovered "The Wall of Shame," the distinct pervasive culture of slow decision making was no longer a mystery. Unfortunately, many of the employees will bring home and model this same style in their personal lives. They are immersed in it day in and day out. It's all they know. It's all they've become.

An illustration of how education can influence decision making is a team of employees I have been coaching for many years now by developing and motivating engineers to be better consultants. Many of my seminars and the time spent on site with the client have been with as many as twenty to thirty engineers at a time. Can you imagine spending eight hours in a classroom with a group of analytically trained individuals? The training sessions have been at times so paralyzed by slow decision making and excessive analysis that some individuals in the presentations have even gone so far as to question what was meant by the word "today" or "if." They constantly want further clarification before answering a simple question. It's similar to Clinton's stonewalling decision making when, in the Monica Lewinsky investigation, he questioned the word "is"! Don't let your educational background prevent you from integrating into your life a more balanced approach to decision making.

In the following section, take the Decision-Making Style Test. Find out where you are on the scale of effective and timely decision making. Discover if it is potentially an asset or barrier to your life and career. There are instructions on how to score the test upon completing it.

✓ DECISION-MAKING STYLE TEST

Respond to each of the following questions. Circle the alphabet letter A, B, or C that best describes your behavior, feeling, or attitude as it actually is, not the way you wish it to be in response to the question. In order to get valid results, you must be absolutely honest!

1. How enthusiastic are you about making a difficult decision?

    a. I'm ready for anything. Good or bad, I live with the outcome.

    b. I'll do it if I have to, but I don't enjoy it.

    c. I can usually avoid it. I know eventually it all works out in the end.

2. Do you generally like taking risks?

    a. I like to take risks. It's a daily fact of life.

    b. I like to take a risk, but I need time to think about it.

    c. There are no guarantees. Why take risks if you don't have to?

3. How do you feel when a decision you've made meets up with disagreement from others?

    a. I know how to defend my point and often still remain friends.

26

b. I first try to keep the peace and hope they will understand.

c. In this case, I usually let someone else have the final say.

4. How important is it to you to live up to others' expectations?

a. It's not very important. I need to be true to myself first.

b. I usually try to please them, but I have my limits.

c. It's very important. I can't risk losing their approval.

5. How analytical are you?

a. I prefer attacking a project. Don't sweat the details.

b. I like to plan most things first. Then I work my plan.

c. Think through everything. Delay answers if you can.

6. How independent are you?

a. I don't mind living alone. I like making my own decisions.

b. I prefer living with someone. I am willing to compromise.

c. My mate makes a lot of our decisions. I like the security.

7. Can you make decisions quickly?

a. I can make up my mind quickly. No regrets here.

b. I need time, but I will eventually get to it.

c. I take my time. If not, I usually mess things up.

8. Do people see you as a positive person?

a. My friends call me the "cheerleader." They count on me.

b. I try to be positive. But sometimes I have to be negative.

c. My role generally is to play "devil's advocate." I'm a realist.

9. When something goes wrong, you:

   a. Immediately apologize and take personal responsibility.
   b. Make excuses for the factors out of your control.
   c. Blame others. It wasn't my idea to begin with.

10. How attached to the old are you?

   a. When I buy new clothes I give my old ones to charity.
   b. My old clothes have sentimental value. Some I keep.
   c. I still have clothes from high school. I keep everything.

You're done . . .

SCORING

Add up your total by using this scoring:
a=10   b=5   c=1

ANSWER KEY

Score 100

Excellent. A perfect score! Your decision-making style is a real asset to your desire for personal reinvention. You've got what it takes to create, plan, implement, and follow any new path you set out to climb. Read the rest of the book and just go and do what you do best. That is—making things happen!

Score 75–99

Very good. You may not have a perfect score, but you are still a timely decision maker. You may run into a mental block at times that may slow you down, but you have the mental strength to go forward and implement change in your life. Watch out for obstacles along the way and assert your decisive powers.

Score 50–74

Good. You've got the potential for being a good decision maker. You have a few weak points to overcome. Some of your areas of improvement may range anywhere from too much of a need to please others and being excessively analytical to being dependent on others and allowing fears to slow you down. You can identify your areas of improvement by rereading the test and comparing your answers to the letter A response for each question. The letter A represents the most efficient implied skills and behaviors needed to be an effective decision maker. Make a list of ways you can improve your decision-making style.

Score 25–49

Below average. Okay, let's be honest. Your decision-making style is probably slow and could be a barrier to your Career ReExplosion. Your areas of improvement may be any combination of the following: too much of a need to please others, excessively analytical, dependent on others, allowing your fears to slow you down, giving in to obstacles, fear of failure, fear of risk taking, and inability to take personal responsibility for outcomes. In the test, the letter A represents the most efficient implied skills and behaviors needed to be an effective decision maker. Make a list of ways you can improve your decision-making style, and act on it.

Score 24 and below

Unsatisfactory. Okay, let's be more than honest. You're stuck in a decision-making style that has been referred to as "paralysis by analysis." Your style is a barrier to Career ReExplosion. Your areas of improvement could be many of the following: too much of a need to please others, excessively analytical, dependent on others, allowing your fears to slow you down, giving in to obstacles, fear of failure, fear of risk taking, and inability to take personal responsibility for outcomes. In the test, the letter A represents the most efficient implied skills and behaviors needed to be an effective decision maker. Make a list of ways you can improve your decision-making style. Consider reading books on decision making. Speak with a counselor. Your style is probably having a visibly negative impact upon various aspects of your life and work.

Medical Issues

Never before in the history of the world have we as a society been confronted more with longevity—planning how to live rather than learning how to die. As a result of modern science, people's lives and careers are being extended well beyond the standard retirement age of sixty-five. In the May 17, 1996, issue of *Science*, Bernard Lakowski and Siegfried Hekimi describe four genes whose mutations are associated with the extension of life span. In their research, they promote a theory that the underlying basis for the aging process is within what they call "Life-Span Clock Genes." Genetic researchers are aggressively at work breaking the life-span code and soon may be extending your life even longer than current projections.

Even without genetic research, modern medicine has extended the average human's life span almost ten years since the prewar era. Breakthrough research in genetics, disease, and pharmacology will continuously raise life expectancy numbers over the next twenty years. Soon, in the 2000s, we may discover living to be well over one hundred years old as commonplace as living to be sixty-five was in the 1960s. Medical longevity breakthroughs have inherent in them a spin-off dilemma: escaping career longevity boredom and the need for reinvention.

The medical community and the media have also made a major contribution to increasing longevity by educating consumers on how to eat properly at home, exercise, quit smoking, and how to make better choices at the restaurant and grocery store. Here are just a few of the many recommendations for longevity successfully being communicated and utilized by our society today.

ILC PRESCRIPTION FOR LONGEVITY

The recommendations listed here have been promoted by the International Longevity Center (ILC), a private group for living a long and healthy life.

1. **Exercise:** Ideally, adults should expend 2,000 to 3,000 calories each week in exercise. Brisk walking, cycling, jogging, or any other intense physical activity can achieve losing this many calories. Everyone should do regular weight lifting to strengthen legs, arms, and trunk.

2. **Weight:** Excessive weight gain at an older age should be avoided.

3. **Diet:** Eat a variety of foods, at least five servings of fruits and vegetables every day. Total fat content: 30 percent maximum of

daily calories. Cholesterol intake: Under 300 mg. Aggressive fat reduction should be avoided, because it is associated with an increase in dietary carbohydrate, which is associated with insulin resistance, and a reduction of "good" cholesterol (HDL) and increase in "bad" (LDL) cholesterol and triglycerides.

4. Microsupplements: Supplements of vitamins and minerals have been shown to reduce the risk of age-related disease. The recommendations per day are:

- Vitamin B_6: 4 mg
- Vitamin B_{12}: 0.01 mg
- Calcium: 1,200 mg (men) and 1,500 mg (women)
- Vitamin C: 200 mg
- Vitamin D: 400 IU (under 70 years) and 600 IU (over 70 years)
- Vitamin E: 200 IU
- Folic acid: 0.40 mg

To reduce risk of heart attack, you should reduce major cardiovascular risk factors. (Source: Dr. Charles H. Hennekens, Harvard Medical School)

- Smoking cessation can decrease heart attack risk by 50–70 percent.
- Maintenance of ideal body weight can decrease heart attack risk by 35–55 percent.
- A 10 percent reduction of total cholesterol can decrease heart attack risk by 20–30 percent.
- Regular exercise can decrease heart attack risk by 35–55 percent.

- A six-point decrease in diastolic blood pressure can decrease heart attack risk by 16 percent.

As it was noted about previous barriers, the biomedical issue can be an asset or an obstacle. Take, for example, the many individuals who up until recently considered serious medical conditions such as cancer and AIDS as an automatic signal to put their lives on hold and in many cases, prepare to die. Then, as new medical breakthroughs came about in each of these fields, the patients who received the new treatments have been either healed or put into remission. Many admit they have found it difficult to shift from a paradigm of preparing to die to a new one of preparing to live.

What's the correlation? There are many. No matter what age you currently are, and whether you know it or not, millennium medicine is definitely creating a career reinvention dilemma for you. As a result of long, youthful, and productive years increasing at an enormous rate, being psychologically prepared to manage career longevity and escape boredom are critical skills needed by everyone in the workforce today. Will you want to be in the same career you are in now when you are sixty, seventy, or eighty? I experienced my first need for reinvention when I was in my twenties. Be assured that millennium medicine will create a need for complete career redirection in 99 percent of the population, in my opinion. For many of them, it will be by the time they reach their forties, fifties, and sixties. Boredom acquired through longevity may account for the single most important driving factor for people in the millennium who want Career ReExplosion.

Don't let biomedical breakthroughs become a modern barrier. Prepare now for the inevitable. By following the steps outlined in this book, you can turn longevity into a physical, emotional, and career triumph. You can acquire a lifetime of reinvention skills beginning to-day.

Technological Issues

Before addressing technology as a potential barrier to Career Re-Explosion, how did we get where we are today? Albert H. Teich, in his book *Technology and the Future*, summarizes it very well. He states:

Each decade in our technological age seems to have its technological icon. [It is] not necessarily the technology that is promoted as having the greatest impact on people's lives, nor that which may ultimately have the most historical significance, but the technology that seems most to capture the public imagination and the spirit of the time.

The 1950s
In the 1950s, it was certainly atomic energy, with the awesome destructive power of the Hiroshima and Nagasaki bombs still fresh in the minds of many and the prospect of "Atoms for Peace" and electricity "too cheap to meter" tantalizingly just around the corner.

The 1960s
In the 1960s, it was unquestionably space, as we raced the Soviet Union to the moon, watched one televised space spectacular after another, gained our first close-up views of the nearby planets, and began to reap the benefits of communications, weather, and remote-sensing satellites.

The 1970s

By the 1970s, we had become disillusioned with many of these technologies and our symbols took on a negative cast. The antinuclear movement and the opposition to atomic power; the worries over resource shortages, the limits to growth and the energy crisis; the growing concerns over environmental pollution; and the somewhat overblown fears (at least in retrospect) of dangerous mutant organisms escaping from gene-splicing laboratories.

The 1980s

While these anxieties did not disappear in the 1980s, they were at least partially overshadowed by the appearance of a new technological icon—the computer, which had evolved by this decade from a room-sized behemoth found only in large organizations to an ubiquitous user-friendly desktop (and laptop) appliance.

The 1990s

And what of the 1990s? There seems little doubt that the technology of this decade is the next stage in computer evolution. [It is] the Internet, and especially the Internet's World Wide Web, the system that has transformed this relatively obscure network once used mainly by scientists and academics into the darling of Wall Street and the popular press.

So here we are in a new millennium where an individual's aptitude for technology determines his or her value to the world of work. In a previous book, *The Top 10 Career Strategies for the Year 2000 and Beyond,* I state that in the millennium, "Social status will be redefined not by education but by the ability to adapt to technology and contribute to society in a rapidly changing information age. Employers will increasingly favor not those with advanced graduate degrees but those with four-year degrees and technical expertise and those with two-year technical degrees. A four-year liberal arts college degree will not become a thing of the past, but knowledge of technology will be the key factor in the hiring process of most corporations."

Is an insufficient knowledge of workplace technology becoming an obstacle to your ability to reinvent yourself? How well have you prepared for future career changes in your life by remaining current with work-related technology? These are important questions to answer. If you believe your skills are not as up to date as they should be, you have a major reinvention problem, and you know the solution. Fix it! It will be virtually impossible in the 2000s to reinvent yourself and remain ahead of the competition without a constant commitment to upgrading your knowledge of workplace technology, no matter how old you are. Don't let this barrier become the one to put the fire out on your next Career ReExplosion.

Company Problems

The last barrier presented here is the company you currently work for or the companies you have worked for in the past. Throughout the 1900s, the company served a good role as big brother, provider, and friend. However, beginning in the 1990s, mergers, downsizing, and the resulting perceived greed has made it an albatross for many. Up until this time period, most derived a single fixed identity from their employer. Basically, people were happy and secure being one-dimensional. They knew that they could be and do the same thing practically forever and would always have a job with their employer.

Times have changed. No longer does the old way of looking at your career work. If you haven't done so already, you need to reevaluate if you are stuck with a single career identity as a result of your current relationship with your employer. Gail Sheehy, in her book *New Passages*, states, "A single fixed identity is a liability today. It only makes people more vulnerable to sudden changes in economic or personal conditions." Sheehy advocates multiple identities for career and life happiness and security. She encourages multiple identities that not only explain what we do but who we are. In my opinion, this is more validation as to why you need to work three Career ReExplosion options at this time in your life instead of just one.

Your unwavering loyalty may have been the standard twenty and thirty years ago, but it is not now. Obviously, there is some measure of loyalty that is necessary, but lifetime commitments are best left for the altar. Corporations have a commitment to the bottom line. I know this is hard to accept, but realize that you are expendable. If companies take care to have a plan to survive and thrive with or without you, should you not be doing the same for yourself?

In your teen and early adult years, your parents, guardians, and your own fickle teenage perceptions of the world dictated who you would become. Now, as an adult, it's time to take your acquired wisdom and decide what *you* want to do. You don't have to rely on your company any longer. It's time to reinvent a new you that will take you through a new phase of your adulthood. This time, you get to decide!

MY PERSONAL BARRIERS TO CAREER REEXPLOSION

As I promised earlier, here is an area to write your personal barriers, or list them on a separate sheet of paper.

1. _____
_____
_____
_____

2. _____
_____
_____
_____

3. _____
_____
_____
_____

4. _____
_____
_____
_____

5. _____
_____
_____
_____

6. _____
_____
_____
_____

7. _____
_____
_____
_____

8. _____
_____
_____
_____

9. _____
_____
_____
_____

10. _____
_____
_____
_____

CHAPTER 3

Return to Your Dreams

WHEN I was a child, I had had lots of wonder and interest in my world just like most children do. In hindsight, a lot of my enterprising tendencies can be traced back as far as preschool. As a five- and six-year-old, I had my own summer lemonade stand, helped organize a monthly block club that guaranteed Pay Day candy bars at every meeting, and helped put together our own neighborhood circus. The circus was a major undertaking filled with attractions, family dog tricks, games, and refreshments. At that age, I felt I could do anything. One day I even believed I could single-handedly burrow a hole from beneath the weeping willow tree in our backyard all the way to China. From a very early age I can recall being driven with dreams and aspirations. I had lots of them.

1

Remember your childhood dreams. Recall the things that interested you as a child.

Now that you get to decide upon your new career, go back to where it all began: your childhood. Here are some important clues as to what will make you very happy today. By paying a visit to your childhood, you may discover other dimensions to your life that will become the source of your next Career ReExplosion.

In the Childhood Dreams and Interests Exercise, recall many of the things that caused wonder and interest in your life in your childhood years. Many of them probably got lost or put aside as you became older. The challenge in this time-of-reflection exercise is to keep it simple. The more simplistic your recall becomes, the more productive this exercise will be.

When I completed this same exercise, I had to recall many simple things that indicated a lot about what I could be doing with my life today. For instance, I have an obscure memory of writing poetry for my fourth-grade teacher, Mrs. Simpson, who I had an enormous crush on. She praised my work, I received recognition, and to this very day because of it, I like to write. Also, I recalled that I joined school choir in second grade, and by the eighth grade, I expanded my musical knowledge by studying guitar and piano. Since that time, I have written lyrics, composed music, and have copyrighted many original songs. In a different memory, I recalled helping my father in the garden each spring. From him I learned to share a love for the earth, and to this very day, have a decent understanding of growing vegetables, flowers, hedges, orchards, and even trimming trees. As I searched for the simple things, I realized my list could go on and on. Before beginning the exercise, here is a Sample Childhood Interests List to help get you focused in the right direction.

SAMPLE CHILDHOOD INTERESTS LIST

- Planting a garden

- Playing a particular sport

- A particular vacation

- Remodeling your family's house

- Camping

- Building a canoe, car, or model plane

- Caring for a family pet

- Being in a school play

- Climbing trees

- Liked rebelling more than conforming

- Favorite teachers

- Favorite classes

- Influential films, movie stars, world leaders, and other celebrities

- Games you played at recess

- Photography club, speech, theater, and other clubs

- Best friends and why?

- School project

- Community project

- Favorite celebration and holiday

Now it's your turn to take a trip down memory lane. Complete the following exercise at your own pace.

CHILDHOOD DREAMS AND INTERESTS EXERCISE

Instructions: In this exercise, recall as far back as you can remember childhood experiences, situations, events, hobbies, interests, rituals, skills, education, and more. Recall the things that made you happy. Use additional paper so that you may be able to fully exhaust your answers. Try not to stop at ten. Good luck!

1. _____
   _____
   _____

2. _____
   _____
   _____

3. _____
   _____
   _____

4. _____

_____

_____

5. _____

_____

_____

6. _____

_____

_____

7. _____

_____

_____

8. _____

_____

_____

9. _____

_____

_____

10. _____

_____

_____

Use the information you just completed as a springboard to isolate potential Career ReExplosion opportunities. Before doing that, however, there is one other set of dreams you need to consider and draw from before making some initial decisions on where to proceed from here.

✦ 2

Identify your current dreams. What passions, skills, and interests have you acquired as an adult?

At the age of forty, I acquired the learned passion of playing ice hockey. Prior to that, I had never watched or played a game of ice hockey in my life. Within four years, I became a licensed USA Hockey referee and completed its coaching program as well. This is clearly an acquired adult passion. It was not something I did as a child. About eight years ago, I decided I was going to learn to cook. I began to rent cooking training videos from the local library. I taught myself how to cook. This, too, is an example of an acquired adult passion or skill.

As long as it is something you truly enjoy and you acquired a love for it within your adult years, please list it in the following exercise. Also include in the following exercise your favorite skills and strengths you have acquired through your work. Examples of this could be public speaking, presentations, training, networking, selling, human resources, marketing, and more.

CURRENT DREAMS
AND INTERESTS EXERCISE

Instructions: In this exercise, list acquired adult experiences, situations, events, hobbies, work interests, rituals, skills, education, and more. As an adult, consider the things that make you happy. Use additional paper so you may be able to fully exhaust your answers. Try not to stop at ten. Good luck!

1. _____
_____
_____

2. _____
_____
_____

3. _____
_____
_____

4. _____
_____
_____

5. _____
_____
_____

6. _____

   _____

   _____

7. _____

   _____

   _____

8. _____

   _____

   _____

9. _____

   _____

   _____

10. _____

   _____

   _____

Here is where the fun begins. Place both lists side by side if your responses are on separate sheets of paper. In the following exercise, list your Top Ten Dream Careers that may be derived from the dreams, passions, and experiences you have accumulated from the two lists. Brainstorm! There are no right or wrong answers. Use the Internet and type in key words from your list into one of the search engines. Browse on the World Wide Web, read, and put time into the next exercise. Be extremely creative. Do not base your answers on required resources, money, or education. Base your answers solely upon desire. Have fun!

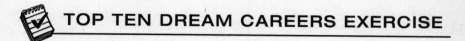

TOP TEN DREAM CAREERS EXERCISE

Instructions: In this exercise, list the top ten fun careers that can be derived from your two previous dream lists. Remember, do not create your answers based on a need for money or resources. Money aside, create a list of careers solely from the things that make you happy. Use additional paper in order that you may be able to fully exhaust your answers. Have fun!

1. _____

_____

_____

2. _____

_____

_____

3. _____

_____

_____

4. _____

_____

_____

5. _____
_____
_____

6. _____
_____
_____

7. _____
_____
_____

8. _____
_____
_____

9. _____
_____
_____

10. _____
_____
_____

3

Diversify! Choose three Career ReExplosion options that will make you happy.

In the past, being one-dimensional in your career was more than likely what had stifled your potential for Career ReExplosion. The goal now is to make you multidimensional. From the top ten list, select now your Top Three Career ReExplosion Options. The options you select now become the basis for your new commitment to being multidimensional. Developing three options now instead of one will also help prevent any future danger of job lock. Keep in mind that these three choices are fluid. They can evolve, change, or be exchanged for something completely new from your list a week, a month, or even years from now. The important thing is to take action now and start somewhere. Begin with these three choices and commit to pursuing them passionately.

Okay, so what are your three Career ReExplosion choices? What did your research and reflection uncover? List them here so you can proceed to subsequent steps.

TOP THREE CAREER REEXPLOSION OPTIONS

1. _____

2. _____

3. _____

4

In your disbelief, believe you can do it.

Upon looking at the choices you've listed, you may already be having some disbelief about the reality of it all. Don't worry; it's normal to have doubts. However, in your disbelief, you need to proceed as if you believe you will succeed. You don't have to wait until you are mentally there. In fact, don't wait. If you do, you'll never launch your ship. Even two thousand years ago, the biblical account of Doubting Thomas speaks volumes on this exact dilemma. As the story is recorded in the New Testament, Thomas, despite eyewitness reports of the resurrection, remained skeptical. At one point, Thomas encounters an apparition behind closed doors in an upper room. He then speaks a phrase that has inspired two millennia of generations. He states, "Lord I believe, help me with my disbelief."

From this point forward, all you have to do is commit to proceed to believe in your disbelief and take the appropriate actions outlined in this book. A complete and total convincing belief will come at a later time. All you need is a willingness to take small and strategic steps from this point on. Are you willing to take these small but significant steps? If the answer is no, whether you know it or not, you're setting yourself up for failure. If the answer is yes, you can go wherever you want to go and you will succeed at whatever it is you want to do.

5

Surround yourself with family and friends who will believe with you.

Your core family—individuals such as a spouse, children, father, mother, life partner, and close friends—has a great deal of influence on the career path you have taken up until now and will take in the future. A parent or spouse, for example, may have pushed you into a lucrative career because of the money you could make. All the while, your love for other things such as art or music were ignored.

A neighbor from years ago, who we'll call Jack, expressed this exact frustration with his parents. Jack's parents were wealthy immigrants. They had spent a lot of money preparing their only child for a dream money career. At their request, he became a doctor specializing in gynecology. Consider his comments:

I hate what I do. But I have no way out. I love my parents too much
to disappoint them. My father passed away last year, and I'm the
only thing that keeps my mother happy. "My son the doctor," she
says all the time to her friends. To make matters worse, I've ended
up an ob-gyn, I think I'm gay, and I'm getting married next year
because I can't break my mother's heart by not going through
with it.

As it is for Jack, family may be an overwhelming topic for you. If you're like him, you probably find it easier to cave in to their expectations and actually place your own happiness on hold. Joyce Schwartz, in her book *Successful Recareering*, agrees. "Many people just get worn down by their family's nagging. And they cave in." One of her clients said, "My dad was a lawyer and so was my grandpa. I couldn't get out of it." Another stated, "Mom had dreamed her whole life I'd be a doctor."

Judy, a close friend of mine for many years, was basically told by her fiancé that he would not marry her until she terminated her employment as a flight attendant for United Airlines. His influence was powerful enough and her inner guidance system was weak enough that she immediately quit her job. Later, while raising seven children, she had an opportunity to grow a career as a professional vocalist. Through his influence, he destroyed this career opportunity as well.

There is another classic example of family intervention into a person's Career ReExplosion in the book, *The Best Work of Your Life*. In it the authors state, "One fellow found an original approach. He talked his wife into having another baby, and now they have a very real reason for not rocking the career boat."

Take a moment now to determine how your core family may attack your career goals and crush your desire for personal success. Answer the following questions: How has your family helped or hurt your career choices? Who are you living your career for, your spouse, mother, father, or someone else? How can you achieve your own goals and objectives while still getting along with your family? Take a moment to answer these questions now.

Please keep in mind that no one is denying that your spouse, parents, and loved ones are very important. However, when it comes to your own personal Career ReExplosion, you must love yourself first; then you will be able to love those closest to you and contribute in a valuable way to their lives. Here are some steps that you can take to create a balance between your family relationships and your personal career goals and decisions.

STEPS TO BALANCING CAREER GOALS AND FAMILY

- Compromise in other areas with your family. Make some concessions in aspects that do not affect your career, but do not give in to their demands for your life and career.

- Talk to your father and/or mother. Have adult-adult communication. Honor them by thanking them for their opinion. Then go and do what you think is best for you.

- After explaining yourself to your family once or twice, keep all future conversations light. Talk about the weather if you have to.

- Surround yourself with like-minded, innovative, creative, and positive people.

- Get advice from books like this one and listen to it.

- Speak with a professional counselor.

6

Eliminate friends who do not support your Career ReExplosion aspirations.

Family you cannot choose, but friends are a choice. If you want to soar like an eagle, you can't dine with turkeys. Take inventory of your friends now. How many of them are cutting-edge role models, energetic, creative, well-read, risk-takers, curious, and inspirational?

How many of them are high-maintenance, negative, toxic, and bring you down? To protect the guilty, you don't have to write that list down.

Once you know who the destructive friends are in your life, run, don't walk, from them. Don't confront them about their negative attitude or destructive energy. They need to come to their own realizations, and anything you say is not going to help them do it. Don't try to change them. Just run.

Is this cruel? No. There is no reason to entertain negative friends in your life unless you get some ego boost from knowing that you are better than the poor souls you baby-sit all the time. Spend your free time with friends who are more talented, who inspire and challenge you, and from whom you can learn something.

Remember that you're an adult. It's time to play by adult rules. You're the leader, and you make your own choices. Don't ever forget it.

Chapter Review

1. Remember your childhood dreams. Recall the things that interested you as a child.

2. Identify your current dreams. What passions, skills, and interests have you acquired as an adult?

3. Diversify! Choose three Career ReExplosion options that will make you happy.

4. In your disbelief, believe you can do it.

5. Surround yourself with family and friends who will believe with you.

6. Eliminate friends who do not support your Career ReExplosion aspirations.

CHAPTER 4

Set the Stage

Now that you have isolated three dream careers, the time has come to set the stage for one or all of them to become a reality. Remember, the reason why you selected three is because you don't want to put all your eggs in one basket. We stated earlier that the lack of being multidimensional is what got you into job lock in the first place. The other reason is because success is a numbers game. It's more likely that one of three pursuits will be successful for you than if you pursued only one.

7

Rekindle your childhood curiosity for trying new things.

The first thing you can do to embark on your dream career is to rekindle your childhood curiosity for trying new things. Essentially, commit to getting out of your comfort zone.

A few years ago, while writing *The Top 10 Career Strategies for the Year 2000 and Beyond,* I took a break from many weeks of writing. I got completely out of my comfort zone. I drove into the parking lot of the Florida Panthers Ice Hockey Club. I had never seen an ice hockey rink in my life. Within ninety minutes, I had purchased a pair of Bauer 5000 ice hockey skates, skated on them, and scheduled private lessons with a coach, all before I left. Talk about the importance of experiencing and trying new things! Every time I am inside an ice arena, it is so foreign to what I usually do that I still can't believe I'm there. Those who read my previous book, *Start Your Own Business in Thirty Days,* know that this curiosity paid off. I eventually turned a hobby into a small business I call the American Hockey Association.

The three dream careers that you selected are probably so new to you that you'll need to get out of your comfort zone and begin to start trying anything related to them. One individual I know wanted to become a paid ice hockey instructor so badly that he gave the lessons away for free until he had acquired a reputation worthy enough to begin charging.

8

Be creative and unconventional.

In order to set the stage for you to launch your Career ReExplosion, get ready to be creative and unconventional in every way. Every week and every day, get totally crazy. For instance, jump on an airplane and visit that city you've always wanted to live in. Schedule yourself for a week or weekend of seclusion and self-discovery at a five-star hotel or in a tent in a national park. Make that phone call to the person or celebrity that you think can help you. Go to the library or log on to the Internet and just get lost in your dream careers' subject matter.

The above list could go on and on. Get creative with your newfound dream careers. If you are willing to let your creativity flow, you will have the fuel you need later to successfully launch them. Get crazy, and have a lot of fun.

9

Identify transferable skills.

Here is some really good news. Part of Career ReExplosion is actually embarking upon the familiar. Breathe a sigh of relief. This is the easy part. Look deep inside yourself for skill sets that you currently are proficient at and that can be easily transferred into any one of your new career options. Transferable skills are more about who you are than what you do. Knowledge of these skills places you in the driver's seat. Identifying and acknowledging these skills makes you more of a veteran than it does a rookie in your new career.

I experienced the power of transferable skills when I started the American Hockey Association. Although I had never played hockey before, I utilized acquired skills to run the company more than I did the new skills of playing ice hockey. To run the company, it took the transferable skill of entrepreneurism, which I had. It also took my innate love for sales and marketing to promote it. And in order to work on the ice as a referee and coach, it took communication and training skills that had been a major part of my career responsibilities for many years. In something as foreign to me as ice hockey, I remain in wonder as to how much of my past is at work in one of my present career reinventions. The author of the Old Testament book, Ecclesiastes, said it well: "There is nothing new under the sun." There *is* nothing new. You have all that you need to be successful already, right inside you. You just need to identify what your current transferable skills are in the next exercise and begin using them to make your dream career come true.

 ## TRANSFERABLE SKILLS INVENTORY

Instructions: In this exercise, list ten or more transferable skills you have acquired throughout your life. For example, being a lawyer would *not* be listed as a transferable skill. However, skills that you have developed from childhood on that are transferable would be; for example, communication, public speaking, working with numbers, working with people, liking computers, creative, analytical, detail-oriented, enjoying travel, and more. Use additional paper in order that you may fully exhaust your answers. Try not to stop at ten. Take pride in a well-thought-out list.

1. _____
_____
_____

2. _____
_____
_____

3. _____
_____
_____

4. _____
_____
_____

5. _____
_____
_____

6. _____
_____
_____

7. _____
_____
_____

8. _____
_____
_____

9. _____

_____

_____

10. _____

_____

_____

⭐ 10

Build relationships with mentors and role models.

At various points in my life, I had different mentors and role models who have influenced me just when I needed it. At the age of sixteen, I was very fortunate to have met Leonard Evans. In the book, *Get the Job You Want in Thirty Days*, I share more about the significance of this very important relationship. When we met, Leonard had just completed advanced studies at Princeton Theological Seminary. He and his wife Bette had moved to Ohio and had taken on a pastorate in a small country church not far from my home. I was introduced to him through some friends.

After attending services for a few months, I liked what I heard in his homilies. To the dismay of the church's board of directors (who eventually wanted to get rid of him), he declared from the pulpit routinely, "I hate religion." Well, I did, too, and so did a lot of other people. We had a lot in common. In actuality, he mentored one simple message to me as well as to the many others who were willing to listen to him. It was his belief that all biblical writings, and for that matter, all spiritual writings, pointed to one singular message: love one another. Everything else, in his opinion, was sweating the details.

Leonard passed away on Palm Sunday in 1998. He will always be remembered as a powerful personal mentor. I was his protégé for many years. He coached me with most of the life skills and people skills I use to this very day.

Later, I acquired role models and mentors while working at People Express Airlines. Many individuals like Don, Melrose, Kim, Eric, Colleen, and others I admired, set an example, and I imitated their management styles. They had a positive impact on my life in both the short and long term. Because People Express Airlines screened well and recruited on average one in one hundred applicants, most of my colleagues were brilliant. I learned a lot from them.

To this very day, I continue to have a great mentor relationship with Jorgen Roed, CEO of Scanticon, Scandinavian Conference Center Hotels, originally founded in Denmark. He has had the single greatest impact upon how I effectively perform as a leader. He has also had an impact on how I consult for the CEOs of the many organizations that I currently work for in my consulting practice. Mentors are an important addition to everyone's life. My hope is that if you don't have one, you will now go out and build a mentoring relationship as soon as possible.

Why does a Career ReExploder need mentors and role models? A mentor acts much like a guide and helps you navigate through waters you have never sailed before. If you do not take criticism well, that may be a sign that you are not open to integrating into your life mentors and role models. The ability to accept coaching and guidance is an essential ingredient for long-term Career ReExplosion success. Here is why you need to immediately build relationships with mentors and role models.

BENEFITS TO HAVING MENTORS AND ROLE MODELS

They can . . .

• Teach necessary skills and capabilities in a new field

• Provide you with challenging assignments

• Give you access to key contacts

• Provide feedback when you need to improve

• Offer praise when you are doing things right

• Be a sounding board for ideas

• Get you public recognition for your accomplishments

• Help you set goals

• Give you advice

• Write letters of recommendation

• Be the key to your dream career

• At times, be your only friend

How do you find a mentor? Get out there and get active in your new dream careers. Network! Many successful individuals are willing to help you, once they know who you are. Consider a former boss or a friend that you admire both personally and professionally. In some situations, hiring a mentor/coach may be the way to go. It is well worth the investment.

✦ 11

Do your research.

Before entering a new career, become familiar with its language, its scope, and even some details. Begin to sound like an insider, even though you haven't been there yet. When I started to play ice hockey and started the American Hockey Association, I did not know creases, hat trick, off-sides, checking, forechecking, five-hole, and boarding, to mention a few terms. At one point I was so determined to learn what others had known for more than twenty years that I made flash cards of all the jargon and memorized it while on U.S. Airways traveling to various client offices around the globe. Please take time to do your research and learn as much as you can about your dream careers. Here are valuable research tips that work.

DO-YOUR-RESEARCH TIPS

- Spend time at the public library at least once a week.

- Split some of the time with the local university's library.

- Call, ask to lunch, and talk with professors in your field.

- Get lost in a large bookstore.

- Subscribe to as many magazines as possible, and speed read them.

- Make flash cards to memorize new phrases and terminology.

- Subscribe to trade newsletters.

- Open a file folder on your hard drive for each new career you are researching.

- Clip relevant articles from magazines. Scan and file them on your computer.

- Talk with as many people as you can about your new career.

- Watch and videotape TV shows that are relevant.

- Search the Internet with key words relating to your subject matter.

- Download key articles and save them.

- Join related trade organizations.

- Get invited to parties for learning and networking.

- Attend seminars.

- Buy or rent appropriate videos.

How have the above ideas inspired you to go about implementing your research? When will you begin? Hopefully, today or tomorrow, you will launch your investigation. Remember, although you are in the initial discovery phase, don't see it as a destination. Research in your dream careers is a journey. Consider it a commitment to lifelong learning.

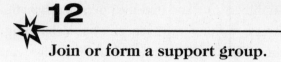

12
Join or form a support group.

This is an easy one. All you have to do is get involved with meeting people who are actively engaged in your new career options. It could be as formal as a group that is already meeting once a month, such as a trade organization. It could also be something informal such as a discussion group that you start out of your own home. Keep in mind that the group does not need to contain a lot of people to be effective; just you and one or two other individuals that have common interests meeting once a month should be sufficient. When you get together, share the events that have transpired over the previous weeks since you last met. You can bet each person will have stories that may save you from potential peril, save you time, money, and provide references for networking and new business opportunities.

You can also achieve your support group needs on line. Get involved in or create a chat room for your new career. Create or participate in a related forum. Make friends on line and exchange support E-mail.

13
Volunteer.

Reevaluate the old notion that you must be paid for work. Igniting your dream careers may mean performing some work for no pay at all. Workers with a traditional mind-set have a big problem with nonpaid work, especially if the work goes on for days, weeks, or even months.

Keep in mind that volunteerism translated into personal benefits to you means free discovery, gaining experience, résumé-building, gathering contacts, and more. What you gain is valuable, though you are not actually being paid. For instance, just the personal benefit of learning something new could cost you thousands of dollars at a university. As an unpaid worker in your dream career quest, you acquire knowledge that you will use later to contribute to your success. You learn new skills and information completely free of charge. Isn't that wonderful? Here are a few ways that you can immediately begin today to volunteer in your new careers and reap the rewards.

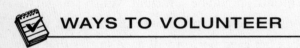 ## WAYS TO VOLUNTEER

- At your current job, after your own work hours, go and help out in a department engaged in your new career interests.

- Call various nonprofit organizations and inquire as to the possibility of working in your area of interest. A good place to start would be to call area religious organizations, hospitals, charitable agencies, public service groups, and more.

- Become an intern. Internships are not just for college students. Most companies would welcome an intern in your area of interest and probably even pay minimum wage while you are gaining knowledge.

- Become an apprentice here or abroad. Many companies would welcome you to come and work for them in a particular area of interest for three to six months. If you have an added interest in

70

travel, the opportunities for apprenticeships in foreign countries are endless.

• Immediately develop your own product line of services, and give it away. Don't wait for someone to pay you before you are willing to work for them. Volunteer your services until you gain months of experience and credibility, which allows you to sell your service product line at a rate in line with current professional fees.

If you would be willing to do it, you could start today or tomorrow researching and getting involved in volunteerism in your dream career. When you do, here are some of the many benefits to you.

 ## BENEFITS TO VOLUNTEERING

- Develop new skills
- Provide a big contrast from your regular work
- New sense of enthusiasm and fulfillment
- Free training
- New friends
- Sense of camaraderie
- Expand your résumé
- Contacts and networking
- Discover role models
- Connect with a mentor
- Experience in a new field
- Recognition
- Use of personal creativity
- References
- Free to excel
- Minimal work boundaries
- Develop leadership
- Overcome boredom

14

Acquire the right credentials.

Volunteering helps you acquire the right credentials. However, acquiring the right credentials also means participating in formal training to have the education you need to excel in your dream careers.

Once they are adults, most people detest attending formal training situations. I recently attended USA Hockey's Coach Certification Program. An acquaintance attended the two-day program with me. He was visibly agitated and uncomfortable sitting in a classroom, and that was just after the first hour of instruction. At the end of the first day, he was already having doubts if he would return the next day for the second session. He was quite verbal about the fact that he did not enjoy being in a classroom learning situation.

Love it or hate it, formal training for credentials is an important part of many dream careers. Just because you may not enjoy training, do not avoid this necessary step. If you were satisfied with your job and career path, you would not be reading this book. Because you really want to open up a new path of opportunity, accept the formal training challenge. Consider the following story of someone who took the formal training challenge to launch his dream careers.

At the age of forty, Hoyt Gier quit a six-figure job in Seattle and moved his family, which included three children, to Hanover, New Hampshire, so he could attend Dartmouth's Tuck School for an M.B.A. Gier's story was reported in the *Wall Street Journal* on April 27, 1999. Although his radical actions puzzled his bosses, family, and even his parents questioned his judgment, Gier couldn't be happier. "Dartmouth exposed me to many business possibilities new to me or previously thought to be out of reach," he says. "The business world looks a lot bigger to me now than it did just a couple of years ago." Upon graduation, Mr. Gier has had to turn down offers to return to his old career in the cement industry with significantly higher pay and authority. He's taken an offer in an entirely new direction: Wall Street.

You do not have to wait to launch your dream career until after your training is complete. In many career reinvention situations, you can begin enjoying your new career today while simultaneously completing any formal training you have deemed necessary as part of your transition plan. David Evans, a thirty-year GM veteran, did just that.

In his story, published in *Newsweek*, February 1, 1999, writer Daniel McGinn states, "What sets Evans apart from others hit by big workplace changes is his enthusiasm for technology, his commitment to self-improvement, and his healthy sense of perspective. On his forty-five-minute commute Evans listens to business audiotapes; at night he pursues a master's degree in systems engineering, even though he is twenty years older than his classmates. Evans' solution for keeping his career current? 'I'm a technologist, but I think the best computers we have are the ones between our ears.'" Like Evans, programming the computer between your ears could be a real boost to remaining current and successful in your dream career.

15

Take personal responsibility.

"As a society, we have handed to others the power of responsibility for a good portion of our lives. Amongst other things, we expect to be provided for if we can't (welfare, unemployment insurance), kept healthy (doctors, pharmacists/chemists), kept safe (policemen, firemen, military), provided for at our retirement (pension funds, government social security), have our career path planned out for us (boss/supervisor), have children cared for and educated (day cares, schools), and have our spiritual sides nurtured (priests, pastors, rabbis)," says Michel Foisy in his article, "The Law of Personal Responsibility" (Version 2) on the Internet at http://www.connectmmic.net/ users/foisy.

Do you know people who live the way Michel Foisy describes in his article? His comments appear to be making the point that people who do not take responsibility for themselves are all around us. For instance, how many individuals do you know who remain in jobs that they don't like because they have said, "The company or boss never promoted me"? How many have said to you that they would be doing something completely different with their life but "my husband/wife does not want me to do it"? How many times have you made similar statements? Taking personal responsibility for your Career ReExplosion is the most important thing you can commit to *right now*.

Foisy agrees. "Do you know anyone who is unhappy at work; someone who has been complaining about their job for years but has done nothing about it? Do you know that person intimately? Could that person be you? In the past, employers took responsibility for providing lifelong employment to an individual. If you needed to be retrained, they would suggest it and get you trained. In today's changing work environment, each individual must take responsibility for their careers. No one is out there looking out for you. There is no more job security. You must provide your own. With the use of computers becoming more and more prominent in the work place, have you been learning how to use them? Do you read trade publications to keep up on the latest trends and direction for your industry or profession? Are you keeping your skills up to date? Again, if you don't do it, no one will do it for you.

"If you don't like your work environment, change employers. No one forces anyone to stay a lifetime in one job for one company. More than half of our waking hours are spent at work. Life is too precious to spend that much time unhappy."

Though we have been raised in a society with socialistic tendencies, in this section, the message is clear: "If it's to be, it's up to me." Please take a moment right now to make a commitment to quit relying on others to create your success. You can do whatever it is you want to achieve. If you can dream it, you can do it. The catch is that you alone are responsible to make it happen. Foisy sums up this section on personal responsibility quite well. "The bottom line is to take personal responsibility for the care of your soul, your body, your financial well being, and all other aspects of your life. You will not regret it."

Chapter Review

7. Rekindle your childhood curiosity for trying new things.

8. Be creative and unconventional.

9. Identify transferable skills.

10. Build relationships with mentors and role models.

11. Do your research.

12. Join or form a support group.

13. Volunteer.

14. Acquire the right credentials.

15. Take personal responsibility.

CHAPTER 5

Build a Bridge

Too often, people don't launch their dream careers because they view it as a dangerous leap across a bottomless pit. On the fear scale, many would rate it up there with speed car racing and parachuting.

In reality, effective career reinvention is as safe and easy as riding a bicycle. It's like the small steps of trial and error you took before you learned how to ride your first bike. Almost anyone can do it. Career ReExplosion is not just for people like Ronald Reagan, who went from screen actor to President of the United States, no more than running is only for joggers. It's for everyone!

16

Write a Career ReExplosion plan and divide it into small active steps.

In order to build a bridge from where you are today to where you want to be, write yourself a plan. The plan, when developed with small active steps, will become your safe passage across what appears to be a bottomless pit. But make no mistake; a good plan with real action provides more than enough stability to help you safely make the leap.

In order for a plan to be effective, it must be specific and filled with action. For instance, I know one individual who relies on spiritual plans from the New Age brand of personal reinvention. She is very unhappy with her current job situation. Her spiritual connection with the universe and a psychic are telling her that it is going to all work out in three to six months. Each psychic has been predicting the same time frame for three years. As a result, she has been waiting for the universe to resolve her unhappiness for more than three years. All the while she "connects" and prays, she has no written action plan, and her technology skills to support a reinvention are not in the '80s, let alone the 2000s.

In the biblical writings of the New Testament, James, in the book of James, takes issue with this type of nonspecific and nonactive existentialism. In his book, chapter 2:17, he declares, "So faith by itself, if it has no works, is dead." In short, if you want to succeed at launching your dream career, you need to have a written plan filled with actions that you actually implement in order to add substance to your faith. The plan needs to be filled with actions that are big and small, achievable, reasonable, and have a strategic and cumulative contribution to your ultimate goal. A lot of people can talk the talk. If you want results, you must be willing to walk the walk. Faith without works is dead!

In case you need examples of what is specific and what's esoteric, I've prepared a list for you below. This should help clarify the next step so that your plan is right on target.

EXAMPLES OF NONSPECIFIC AND NONACTIVE PLANS

(Examples of what your plan should not look like)

- I'll think about it for a week.

- Once they get back to me, I'll decide what to do.

- I need to wait it out at work and see if things get better first.

- After vacation, I'll attack this issue.

- I'll investigate a good business plan software and then proceed.

- I just need to get more aggressive with what I need to do.

- Give me a year, and it will eventually happen.

- My friends have advised me to just sit tight and let it all work out.

- I'm really talented; someone will eventually discover me someday.

- Once I learn more, I'll be better prepared.

- I need to wait until I'm in a better frame of mind.

- When the house and car get paid off, I'll be ready to go further.

- Once I know more, and know the ins and outs, I'll be ready.

- It'll come to me.

- I'll know it when I see it.

- I need more data.

All of the above statements are vague and ambiguous. If you have said them, say them, and unknowingly make them part of your plan, you're going nowhere. Following is a sample Power List of Specific and Active Plans.

POWER LIST OF SPECIFIC AND ACTIVE PLANS

(Examples of what your plan should look like)

- Find at least one mentor in my dream career within two weeks.

- Begin volunteer work and developing new skills by Saturday.

- Have a talk with my family Wednesday night about my new plans.

- Take my parents out to lunch Sunday and ask for their support.

- Enroll in one class tomorrow for next semester.

- One hour of research on the Internet or bookstores daily, starting today.

• Call a friend of a friend by Monday and see if he/she can help me.

• Attend the monthly association meeting.

• Call and network with five contacts a week.

• Rewrite my résumé by Sunday.

• Apply for a part-time job just for the experience and land it within two weeks.

• Call one company a day until I find three to give away my services to in exchange for references in my new career.

All of the above statements are great examples of good content for any action plan that you will begin to write upon completing this section. They work because they are specific, attainable, filled with action, and have assigned time frames for completion. Now it's your turn. After reading items 17 and 18 below, write a two- or three-page plan for each of the three Career ReExplosion ideas you agreed upon in chapter 2. Take your time and keep it simple. Keep the following in mind.

✷17

Divide the plan into two chapters: actions for the immediate present and actions for the immediate future.

As you get ready to write a plan for each of your dream careers, write it as a two-point plan. The headline over the first part of the plan would read, "Actions for the Immediate Present." The headline over the second part of the plan would read, "Actions for the Immediate Future."

Both plans detail your goals and objectives. However, it is important to recognize that there are differences between the two parts of the plan. The plan for the immediate present begins today and spans about a thirty- to sixty-day time period. The plan for the immediate future begins in about thirty or sixty days from now and may run for up to a year from now. By focusing on the immediate present, it encourages you to take primary foundation-building actions that, when implemented properly, place the horse before the cart. The actions in the first part need to be very simple first-step actions. They should be small and basic. The steps should lead you to the more aggressive actions detailed in part two of your plan.

Examples of plans that would be typically included in the immediate present would be actions such as updating your résumé, making a phone call to a particular contact, and establishing a support group of positive friends. In general, the actions are easy to accomplish without ever immersing yourself in your new career as your sole source of income.

Examples of plans that are typically included in the plans for the immediate future would be actions such as completing your first product prototype, securing a part-time or full-time position to gain more experience, a deadline for making your first sales presentation, and a deadline for exiting your current career. In general, these actions may be more difficult to accomplish and may only be achieved if the basics in the first plan were effectively executed. The actions in part two, when implemented, bring you financial independence in your dream career.

WHY DO YOU NEED
TO WRITE A PLAN?

• If you are going to need any amount of seed money to help you make the changeover to your new career, you will want to know how much, how you are going to get it, and how you are going to pay it back whether to yourself or to a lender.

• The mere existence of a plan becomes a daily reminder of your commitment and a constant call to action.

• A plan helps you to define where you are going and how you are going to get there. Nothing as important as a career change should be left to chance.

• A good plan saves you money and time by focusing on results-oriented activities.

• It's hard to take what you are doing seriously if there is little or nothing in writing about your goals. This small plan will be the most important document you will ever prepare to make your Career ReExplosion a reality.

18

Write a one-page introduction to each plan, identifying your vision and mission for your dream career.

I once read the story of an old sea captain who gathered an entire crew of men willing to go off to sea. As they departed the seaport, one of the sailors asked, "Captain, where exactly are we going?" The captain was confident in his own intuitive sense of direction and had no reply. He just expected everyone to rely on his navigational abilities. However, after many days at sea, a storm tossed the ship for a whole night. When the calm came and the light of dawn covered the ship, the captain lay unconscious on the deck. The crew had no idea where to guide the ship. They were unable to agree on a clear direction, and so the crew divided up. They took the lifeboats from the ship and abandoned the captain.

The captain made a horrible error by not establishing a clear and stated mission for the trip. In writing the introduction to your Career ReExplosion plans, write at least one page describing your vision and mission for each plan. It is important to establish a clear purpose so that you know in writing where you are going as well as those who in the future may join you.

YOUR PLAN'S INTRODUCTION

Write an introduction for each plan. In it, answer the following questions:

- Why do I want to do this?

- What do I hope to accomplish in the short term?

- What do I hope to accomplish in the long term?

- How will this help and/or change me?

- How will it help and/or change others around me?

- Would I ever not want to do this?

- What is my exit plan?

- Where is this all leading to?

- What will I do after this?

Unlike the sea captain, don't rely on your own intuition to know where you are sailing with your dream career. Intuition is helpful, but it should play a supplemental role to having a written and well-defined personal vision and mission. Another advantage to having a one-page vision and mission statement is that it provides you with the ability to clearly share your story with others. You are now specially prepared to share your story with those who can help you, such as those with whom you are networking, potential clients, prospects, mentors, and the media.

If you haven't already done so, go ahead and complete writing your dream career plans now. Follow the guidelines for writing the plans as described in items 16 through 18. Be sure to include a good introduction to the plans containing your vision and your mission for each one.

✶ 19

Be flexible and let your plan evolve. The shortest route to where you are going will not always be a straight line.

Now that you have a plan, be flexible. Letting your plan evolve may be the most important challenge you will ever have while living with your own Career ReExplosion decision. It is hard to imagine that the shortest route to where you are going may not be a straight line. Consider the following story shared by Toni Smith, who recently executed a career reinvention.

"Of all the times that I've sought a new career, this one was the worst," states Smith. She is a business professional who had various careers throughout her life and in recent years had taken time off to raise a family. She was anxious to reenter the workforce and for financial reasons had no time to waste. Though frustrated with the thought of reinventing herself, feeling sorry for herself was not an option. Her plan was to get out of the house, enter the world of work and, specifically, get a job in some aspect of sales.

"After two weeks of looking, I accepted a job working in an environment that was like being on another planet. It was far from what I had expected. I started as a receptionist. Stranger yet, the company was in the manufacturing business. Neither was something I had ever done before. My real plan was to be in sales. Was I crazy? Maybe, but not stupid. I saw potential in my being there.

"Sometimes in life you just have to show up," states Toni, in order for your reinvention plans to work out. "After two months as a receptionist, which seemed like a lifetime, and six months as an executive assistant, which seemed like an eternity, I discovered the manufacturing engineers working around me in the office, that their responsibilities included sales. *Sales*, a word that was magic to my ears."

Almost a year into her career reinvention plan to get out of the house, Toni uncovered what she shares to be "a position in the sales/marketing department that had my name written all over it: sales/marketing coordinator. Although I was given the position, it was given to me with apprehension and reluctance. I was going to prove my adversaries wrong with my innate sales abilities."

Toni states, "For a complete month, I was given the task to bring in advertising sponsorship revenue in order to create cost recovery for a new magazine we were publishing. I know no one expected this to happen, but for that month, the largest amount of revenue was brought in by me. I did it within a two-week period. Whether I stay where I am at or go somewhere else, I know I have an exciting career in sales ahead of me. I'm no longer just a housewife."

Smith knows better than anyone about letting Career ReExplosion plans evolve. Her goal was to enter the world of work after raising a family. She wanted to be in sales. Toni exhibited the patience it takes to let a career plan evolve as well as being able to prove herself along the way to make it happen. In response to the almost twelve months it took to allow her plan to evolve and completely come together, Toni states, "I don't have anything profound to say in ending this story, but I will say this: Whenever I think I can't, I believe I can, and *I do!*"

Right now, give yourself permission to be fluid with your plans. Be ready to change part or all of your plans in the weeks and months ahead. How might family and friends perceive changes in your plan? Some may think changing or abandoning a plan is a statement of failure. Is it really?

While letting your plan evolve, there undoubtedly are going to be changes, additions, and deletions. When a spouse, family member, or friend is critical of your changes, smile! It means that you are one of the very few in this world who is doing something extraordinary with your life. Ordinary people rarely get criticized. The reason why they don't is because they're not doing much. They maintain the status quo. They are not doing anything life transforming. You are, so get ready to let your plan evolve, make changes along the way when necessary, and accept criticism as part of being a mover and shaker. Learn to laugh it off.

When you allow your career reinvention journey to take you down alleys, dead end streets, and even onto the superhighways of life, you open yourself to financial rewards and personal fulfillment opportunities normally reserved for the rich and famous. Career ReExplosion is not a neat little package. It's an explosion. It's a violent rebellion against the status quo. Get ready for some collateral damage along the way. That's okay. Part of the explosion may just open up the side of a mountain filled with gold that you otherwise would not have found. Like Toni Smith, a lot of your dream career success plans are based on the very simple formula of just showing up. "Let us imagine that life is a river," states Shakti Gawain, author of *Creative Visualization*. "Most people are clinging to the bank, afraid to let go and risk being carried along by the current of the river. At a certain point, each person must be willing to simply let go, and trust the river to carry him or her along safely. At this point one learns to 'go with the flow' and it feels wonderful."

This brings us to the next major point along the path of successful career reinvention. In order to be successful at implementing your Career ReExplosion plan, reassess the word *failure*. Sometimes you may encounter costly learning experiences, but they are not failures. Only people that are doing something will experience accusations of failure from themselves and others.

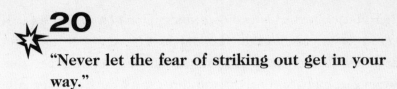

20

> "Never let the fear of striking out get in your way."
>
> —Babe Ruth

Now that you have come this far in Career ReExplosion, you may have awakened in the morning more than once realizing that you are making a major commitment to immediate career reinvention. One part of you may be exhilarated, but another part may be overcome by fear. You may even gulp hard at the thought of it. Yet for others it may even be more dramatic. Suddenly you can't breathe. A panic attack is now in progress! The fear of failure may catch you unaware and suddenly overwhelm you. As each day passes, how will you manage your fears? Will you allow the fear of striking out to destroy your dreams? Or will you pull the covers from over your head in the morning and boldly face the fear head-on and perform the daily actions outlined in your plans?

Beginning now, if you haven't done it already, acknowledge that Career ReExplosion is not easy. At the same time acknowledge that change is a constant and with almost all change will also come a sense of fear. Ask anyone who has gone sky diving for the very first time about fear. Anything new contains an element of fear.

If a new skydiver, for instance, wanted to avoid fear, investing good money in a first jump would not be a good idea. If you wanted to avoid fear, you would not have invested your good money in this book. Change is about fear. It is about exchanging the warm, secure, familiar, and predictable for the unexplored and unpredictable. By pursuing your dream career, you are accepting at this moment that there is nothing familiar about where you are going. Don't let the fear of failure freeze your success. Feel the fear and do it anyway.

Career coach Rosemary Augustine states at her Internet site, http://www.careeradvice.com, the top three fears we face constantly during a career reinvention include:

- Fear of the unknown

- Fear of failure or fear of success

- Fear of rejection

According to Augustine, there are some things you can do to conquer unwanted fear. She states, "Fear of the unknown is the feeling of 'stepping into the abyss,' or any other excuse that keeps us in the 'known.' With fear of the unknown, any change suddenly creates an uncomfortable feeling. Thereby causing you to retreat deeper into the comfort areas of your life. By choosing to step into the so-called abyss, you begin to take steps to 'stretch' outside your comfort zone, expanding it and ultimately creating personal and professional growth.

"Fear of failure and fear of success go hand in hand. You're afraid you will fail and even set yourself up for failure because you don't take the risk to seek your success. Fear of success creates a retreating back versus a moving forward effect, thereby, allowing the fear of failure to take over and impact your success. Once this happens, you become so consumed with the fear of failure that you manifest it. Ultimately achieving that which you fear. Develop your risk taking skills to seek success by learning how to stretch outside your comfort zone.

"Fear of rejection is very common in career transition, and really in all aspects of life. Sales professionals handle rejection daily and most of us figure they're successful because they have developed a tough skin. Maybe they have. But, whether you are a sales professional or not, rejection becomes personal only when you allow it. By not personalizing the rejection, you no longer can feel rejected. Learn to detach yourself from the rejection. This takes some practice, and . . . works . . ."

How do you allow fear to rule your life? How willing are you to fail? Take a moment now to answer these questions. Acknowledge how you have allowed fear and the fear of failure to slow you down in the past. Augustine encourages you to ask yourself some other very important and tough questions about fear as well.

QUESTIONS TO ASK YOURSELF ABOUT FEAR

• Do I recognize the role fear plays in launching my dream career?

• By evaluating my situation, am I aware of the impact fear creates on my success?

• Do I understand why I feel the way I do about fear of the unknown, fear of failure, fear of success, and fear of rejection?

• Am I willing to take the necessary steps to do something about my fears?

• What would happen if I allow fear to rule my life?

In my book, *The Top 10 Fears of Job Seekers*, I lay out a formula for confronting head-on each fear that haunts you. If you choose to run from fear, you have declared its power over you. If you choose to embrace fear and talk about it, you discover that it has no power over you. In *The Top 10 Fears of Job Seekers*, I explain that there is good fear and bad fear. Fear becomes good if it drives a person to become unstuck and to move forward. This book shows you how to embrace your fears, walk directly through them, and utilize them as a source of creativity and innovation. When this happens, fear becomes a positive force. It becomes a powerful fuel for your Career ReExplosion.

Chapter Review

16. Write a Career ReExplosion plan and divide it into small, active steps.

17. Divide the plan into two chapters: actions for the immediate present and actions for the immediate future.

18. Write a one-page introduction to each plan, identifying your vision and mission for your dream career.

19. Be flexible and let your plan evolve. The shortest route to where you are going will not always be a straight line.

20. "Never let the fear of striking out get in your way." —Babe Ruth

CHAPTER 6

Live the Dream Now

FOR some, the road from pro wrestling to politics may seem like a long one. In some ways it may seem farther, longer, and wider than the road to your own Career ReExplosion. Highlighted by NBC in a made-for-TV movie, the network aired *The Jesse Ventura Story* on May 23, 1999. One of the keys to his success is the fact that years before he was elected Governor of Minnesota, Jesse Ventura had begun to care about people. He had embraced caring about others and being a leader long before reality caught up with his career reinvention goal of being a public servant.

The same held true for Sonny Bono who, for most of his career, was viewed by the masses as a has-been pop singer and Cher's other half. Just like many of us, he became pigeonholed as a one-career person. Through a lot of inner determination and goal setting, he set out to prove many people wrong. Prior to his death in 1998, he had aggressively detonated his own Career ReExplosion that the history books will say made him, in the end, a politician very respected by his peers on Capitol Hill. In Sonny's mind he became a leader and a statesman long before it was his reality.

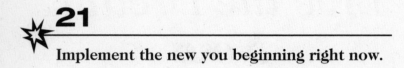

21
Implement the new you beginning right now.

What dream careers did you pick as a result of the exercises in chapter 3? If you're like most, you'll probably make the error of waiting to tell others about the new careers till after you have demonstrated sufficient success and gathered enough documentation to prove it. Also, you may be waiting for your first business cards, letterhead, ID card, or certificate of graduation. Why wait? Where does it say that a person can have a new career only if all the accoutrements are in place? You can maintain your current job and simultaneously launch a multiplicity of new careers all at the same time, simply by declaring it! Wow! That's exciting.

Bruce Marks agrees. He was an advanced-degree finance wizard when he began to simultaneously live out his dream career as an ice hockey coach and instructor. He states, "As a young adult, my parents were insistent that education came first and that I should concentrate on my studies rather than play college hockey. I took their suggestion, studied hard, and received a graduate degree in finance. I chose banking as a profession and headed out into the workplace."

After a ten-year banking career, Marks reinvented himself by starting his own consulting firm. That singular reinvention was not enough. While starting the consulting practice, he began to hang out around an ice rink in his spare time. One day, a rink manager asked if he would assist the staff by instructing some skaters. Marks comments, "Although I had been skating and playing hockey for twenty-five years, I never had experienced teaching someone how to skate or play ice hockey." Without any experience or knowledge of teaching hockey, Bruce Marks immediately began to act like a hockey instructor while still being a highly paid employee of his business consulting firm.

"I took the teaching hockey challenge very seriously," states Marks. "I decided that if I were to become a skating and hockey instructor, then I better get some formal training. I found out who were the best instructors and invested approximately $8,000 to train with these individuals. While I was teaching, I achieved my goal by gaining the knowledge and the tools necessary to teach winning ice hockey and power skating."

Like Marks, no matter what your dream careers may be, you can start hanging out in them and safely rely on the old rule that 99 percent of success in life is just showing up. Start doing today whatever it is that you always dreamed of doing with your career. Do it with or without pay. Over time you can perfect your new career, but that should not hold you back from doing it now. Bruce Marks agrees. "Although my initial teaching style was not as good as it is now, the important thing was that I did not fear starting somewhere, even without experience. Now my advanced training, reputation, and the number of students wanting skating lessons has grown so rapidly that I often find myself skating seven days a week. Over the past two years, I find myself spending more time at the ice rink than I do at my consulting practice!"

As I stated in a previous book, *Start Your Own Business in Thirty Days*, when I reinvented myself into being a training consultant for hotels and restaurants, I embarked on something that I had never done before. The very first action in the Career ReExplosion plan of starting my consulting business was to write a course called *TipsPlus*. The course is designed to help food servers increase their tips through effective service techniques. The minute I began writing the course, in my mind I was a corporate training consultant although I had never done it before. If someone asked me at a party what I did, I said I was a training consultant for the hotel and restaurant industries. I wrote the product at night after selling computers all day for Harris Corporation. The first three contracts for *TipsPlus* I gave away in order to quickly and easily validate my new career. I charged later, but initially the strategy was to give it away to gain training, experience, references and, most of all, better self-confidence in my new dream career.

✴ 22
Restructure your time and priorities.

In order to restructure your time and priorities, you first need a clear idea of how you currently use your time. The following Personal Time Survey will help estimate how much time you currently spend in typical activities. This helps to get a better idea of how much time you have to invest in cultivating your dream careers and where you need to change your priorities. The exercise also helps you identify time wasters that rob you of the extra time necessary to juggle your current job with your new reinvention plans.

THE PERSONAL TIME SURVEY

Instructions: The following survey shows the amount of time you spend on various activities. When taking the survey, estimate the amount of time spent on each item. Once you have this amount, multiply it by seven. This will give you the total time spent on the activity in one week. After each item's weekly time has been calculated, add all these times for the grand total. Subtract this from 168, the total possible hours per week. The result is the number of hours you have to time-manage and prioritize your personal Career ReExplosion.

Activity	Hours per Day	X 7 =	Hours per Week
1. Sleep		X 7 =	
2. Grooming		X 7 =	
3. Eating and preparing food		X 7 =	
4. Commuting		X 7 =	
5. Functions: church, clubs, etc.		X 7 =	
6. Chores, errands, gym, etc.		X 7 =	
7. Working, overtime, homework		X 7 =	
8. Socializing, dating, TV, etc.		X 7 =	
		Total hours per week =	
		Subtract total hours per week from 168 =	
		That number represents the hours you have under current conditions for Career ReExplosion	

What is the total number of hours available to you under current conditions in order to execute your dream career plans? How satisfied are you with that number of hours? If you're like most, there are probably not enough hours left to effectively launch your dream career action plans. You need to start chopping.

As a result of this important exercise, you can see the value of reorganizing and prioritizing your time and activities in the days and weeks to come. Please go back to the above exercise with a red pen or pencil. Make changes to the activities and hours that would increase the time necessary to dedicate focused and consistent energy into your Career ReExplosion.

A good place to begin cutting hours is at your present job. By all means provide your current employer with an honest day's work. However, don't allow the trap of constant overtime be your excuse for not pursuing your dream career. If you continue overtime as a way of life and never get to your new career plans, whose fault is it? Many will blame their employer. It's not. In reality, your commitment to overtime is potentially a way of hiding behind the fact that you are unwilling to do what is difficult and necessary to change your life. Of course, many are not willing to admit that, and so many blame employer demands on their time as the number-one reason for never changing their career.

One gentleman just like this, I have known for more than ten years and through three different employment situations. I will call him Bob to protect his identity. Each time I speak with him, no matter the year, company, or job title, he is deluged with overtime. In his heart he believes that for the past ten years three employers have all controlled his life with overtime. They have somehow jointly plotted to leave him with little opportunity for personal and professional pursuits beyond his career. As I have observed Bob, he works the same fourteen hours a day of overtime no matter the employer. How possible is it three employers all share the same culture of fourteen hours per day of overtime? I don't think so. Is it Bob's *choice* to continually work excessive amounts of overtime for whatever reasons, robbing himself of other pursuits including proper diet and exercise? Personally, I believe the latter is the correct answer. If you are like him in any way, you need to make a commitment to yourself today to work a maximum forty-five hour week, get in thirty minutes a day of exercise time, and spend the rest of the time working on the plan you wrote in chapter 5. You need to take personal responsibility for your time, your dream career, and ultimately yourself. If you don't, who will?

Excessive work habits may not be the only time robbers you may need to change. How much leisure and TV time do you consume? How willing are you to curtail it in exchange for short-term loss and long-term gain? Success researchers have discovered that successful people share in common one major personality trait. They are able to delay gratification. In my last book, *Start Your Own Business in Thirty Days*, I share the story of a woman who, when starting her own business, totally eliminated frivolous spending the complete first year of the business's start-up. She did not consume any entertainment, eliminated dining out, and literally lived on a diet of peanut butter, beans, and rice. In order to gain more hours to launch your dream careers, you *will* have to delay gratification. How willing are you to restructure your time and possibly even temporarily eliminate fun and leisure activities? If you are willing, take some time to rewrite the Personal Time Survey and eliminate activities that will create plenty of hours to manage your action plans in the weeks and months to come.

23

Ask for the help of others and get them involved.

Louie Salaben moved to South Florida from Cleveland, Ohio, in 1989 and lived in a one-bedroom apartment near the railroad tracks. Upon arrival, he immediately acquired a job working in banking, an industry he had been working in for seven years. Unfortunately, an established career in banking was not an asset to Salaben. He felt the pay scale in banking was poor, the responsibilities overwhelming, and the long hours behind a desk tedious. He devised a career reinvention plan, and as part of it he decided to seek out the help of a trusted friend: me.

Louie states, "I shared my situation with Gary, who was not only a friend but an experienced career coach. He took the time to sit down with me and explore my options. We brainstormed for hours. We made lists of what I liked and disliked as well as things I enjoyed doing and things I did not enjoy doing. When we finished, we then compared the two lists. After careful review, we discovered that real estate was emerging at the top of every list. It was through soliciting a friend's involvement in my life that I was able to determine my dream career, how to make more money, and the actions to get me there.

"Within fourteen hours of Gary's involvement, help, and advice, I registered into night school with the Century 21 Real Estate Academy. I had my real estate license within six months. For a few months, I maintained my old job while I built up my new career working hard evenings and weekends. Now, after more than ten years full-time in my new career, I am much happier, take vacations when I want, have no bosses, and make more money than I ever dreamed was possible.

"I am grateful that I took the time and effort to go to a friend's house, got him involved in a very personal aspect of my life, and for the assistance he gave me in helping me succeed. As a friend, Gary was a key resource at one of the most important crossroads in my career. It took both a respected professional and an understanding friend to bring out my real desires and help me reach my full potential."

Salaben discovered that asking for help and getting others involved is a real key to dream career success. As a friend I was happy to be there for him. However, Louie gets all the credit for his success. He had the wisdom to seek out advice and to ask for help. Unlike Salaben, some people have fears that prevent others from becoming involved in their career issues. Here are some of the top fears of involving others that you may experience while executing your Career ReExplosion.

 ## THE TOP FEARS OF INVOLVING OTHERS

- Don't think they are qualified.

- Don't want to impose on them.

- Would owe them a favor in exchange for their help.

- Think I have to do whatever they tell me to do.

- Don't want to disappoint them if I don't take their advice.

- Sign of personal weakness to get others involved.

- Leaves me feeling vulnerable by sharing personal aspects of myself.

- Don't want people knowing about my private life.

- If I tell someone my dreams, I may feel accountable to fill them.

- I may get the wrong advice.

- People may think I'm stupid if I can't figure it out myself.

There may be more reasons, but you have the idea. In spite of all the fears you may have about actively involving others in your dream career plans, the reality is you need their advice and assistance. "No man is an island," the saying goes. There are genuinely people out there who would like to help you. We are all interconnected, and to succeed, we need each other. How will they know you need help unless you swallow your pride and ask them? Take risks to talk to people and find individuals that genuinely care about helping you. When they do, show your appreciation with a thank you note and small, well-thought-out gifts. Some day very soon, when you succeed, someone may need your help and you'll be able to return the favor.

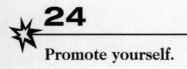

24

Promote yourself.

As Golda Meir once said, "Don't be humble; you're not that great." Detonating your own Career ReExplosion is a time for standing on the mountaintop and shouting who you are and who you are becoming. Tell everyone. Tell the world. If you have joined up with a monastic order and taken a vow of humility, you're off the hook on this one. It's understandable that you abhor self-promotion if you're currently the member of a monastery. If you're not, read on.

In order to succeed in your new dream careers, you need to self-market shamelessly. Every day tell everyone you meet what you're doing, where you are going, what your plans are, what you have achieved thus far and, most important of all, contact the media and have them scheduled for various appearances so you can tell your story to the world. Sound crazy? I hope not. Just look around you, and notice that every product imaginable aggressively promotes its way to success every day. You and your dream career together are a product. Promote them aggressively.

Just a few days ago I was on a flight from Philadelphia to Fort Lauderdale. While stretching my legs in the front of the cabin, I initiated a conversation with a gentleman standing a few feet away. I asked him about his travel and his work. He is the CEO of manufacturing facilities with plants in various parts of the U.S. I asked him what his key leadership challenge is at the moment. He said it was customer service. I gave him my business card immediately. I promoted to him the fact that developing effective customer service for large companies has been my area of expertise for the past fourteen years. Before leaving to go back to our seats for landing, I offered to immediately come and take a look at his operation and help him solve his service problems. He expressed appreciation that I took the effort to talk to him and provide him with a valuable contact. The ability to take initiative and to strike up a conversation with anyone who will listen is vitally important to your self-promotion and long-term success.

In word and deed you need to become a walking advertisement for who you are and what you do. The only way to develop self-marketing confidence is to do it. Do what you fear most, and you will overcome the fear. As a result of becoming effective at self-promotion, you will develop confidence in other areas of your life as well. In actuality, it is more exhausting trying to be humble than it is to take on the daily task of promoting yourself. Here are the ten biggest mistakes people make about promoting themselves.

TOP MISTAKES PEOPLE MAKE IN PROMOTING THEMSELVES

1. Not doing it

2. Being inconsistent

3. Not attending networking functions

4. Turning down public speaking opportunities

5. Not cultivating key relationships

6. Avoiding the media and not developing those relationships

7. Thinking that it is morally wrong to promote themselves

8. Afraid of what others will think if they toot their own horn

9. Not having read books on sales and self-marketing techniques

10. Failure to realize they are a product

11. Not taking initiative to introduce themselves

12. Not having a business card available at all times

13. Telling others they are shy

14. Lacking the trained ability to create conversation and ask good questions

Now that you know it's okay to brag, make a decision to tell at least two people a day about the new you and the various aspects of your dream career plans. Just think, at the end of one year, you will have promoted yourself to 730 people. That's powerful! If just 2 out of 730 people help you; think about how much farther ahead you will be with your new career plans and goals at the end of one year. How much farther ahead will you be if 100 out of 730 people help you?

25

What you speak is what you get.

One of my favorite success stories is that of Arnold Palmer, one of the greatest golf pros of all time. Although I shared his story in a previous book, *The Top 10 Career Strategies for the Year 2000 and Beyond*, it merits sharing again briefly. As the story is told, when Arnold Palmer was ten years old, he used to pretend that he was playing in national tournaments. He went as far as pretending to be a sports commentator announcing, that "the *champion*, Arnold Palmer, is now ready to tee off." Already, at a very young age, Palmer discovered the power of speaking reality into existence. Within ten years of those words, his childlike faith transformed speech into reality.

Through my career seminars and thousands of hours in business consulting, it has been my experience that most people are reluctant to state and believe in who they are until they actually see it happen. In order for you to successfully reinvent yourself, it actually works in reverse. You must first publicly declare the new you and what it is you are becoming long before you may have visible signs that you have achieved it.

Donald Trump utilized the power of speech to create something out of nothing when he conceived Trump Tower on New York's Fifth Avenue. Long before he had built the building or even completed its financing, he had already declared for the world to hear that when completed, Trump Tower would be the number-one address to live in the world. And you know what? Long before it was even built, people were flocking to his doorstep wanting to be a part of something that did not even exist. They were dropping millions of dollars on something they had never seen. Now, that is the power of speech!

In Judeo-Christian philosophy, words are portrayed as extremely powerful tools, as they are in other ancient writings as well. In the Old Testament for instance, in the book of Genesis, the first chapter's story of creation states that "God spoke" and all that is came into existence. Words are portrayed as powerful in the New Testament biblical writings, too. In the Gospel of John, the first chapter states, "In the beginning was the Word." We know that after the discovery of the Dead Sea

Scrolls in the late 1940s, many of the biblical writings such as the ones stated above are carbon dated as far back as four thousand years ago. The power of the spoken word has been known for more than four thousand years. Consider the power of the spoken word in your Career ReExplosion. In the beginning, create through your words. What you speak is what you get.

The next time you are out in public or at a party and someone asks you what you do for a living, what are you going to tell them? Hopefully, by now you know the answer to that question. By all means tell them about who you are now in your new dream career. Why describe to them the same old box you've been living in for the past months and years? You're not that anymore. Tell them the new story about the new you. Spice up your life, live on the edge, and start telling people about Career ReExplosion. Not only do you make the conversation more interesting, more importantly, each time you speak about your dream career, your words contain the power to create the reality you desire. Isn't that exciting? Or as my one mentor, Leonard Evans, would say, "Ain't it fun!"

Chapter Review

21. Implement the new you beginning right now.

22. Restructure your time and priorities.

23. Ask for the help of others and get them involved.

24. Promote yourself.

25. What you speak is what you get.

CHAPTER 7

Take Action

STEVE Leek worked as a senior executive for Edison Brothers Stores, Inc., in the Menswear Group that included the popular retail stores Oaktree, J. Riggings, Coda, and Jeans West. He advanced to the level of vice president after ten years with the organization. In hindsight he states, "During the prosperous years of the company, I became very comfortable with my career at Edison Brothers. I occasionally entertained the idea of leaving. I knew I could be making a much higher salary if I would just make the move to another company. As time went by, I became too comfortable, less challenged, and became more and more disenchanted with my career."

Leek decided it was time to take action. "It was time to take control of my own future," he states. "I immediately began plans with a business acquaintance of mine to start a new business concept. The new business required raising private investment capital while buying time in my current career. We took swift action by developing our business plan by working evenings and weekends aside from my current job. It wasn't easy. We had a long road to travel in order to sell our idea to potential investors. Meanwhile, I was fearful that the word would get out at work that I would soon be leaving. I thought for certain that I would be asked to leave the company. To my surprise, instead, they asked me to stay on as long as possible." Leek, through taking action with enormous amounts of courage, has effectively detonated his own Career ReExplosion. He has become the president and COO of Creativworks, LLC, the country's first network of franchised, retail-based advertising and marketing agencies.

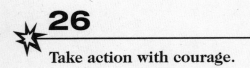

26

Take action with courage.

Talk is cheap, the saying goes. How many people do you know who sit around at work or call you on the phone threatening to make a change in their unhappy cubicle of work? How many people do you know who talk tough and yet take little action? It has been my experience that many career-challenged employees talk the talk of Career ReExplosion, but few have the courage of Steve Leek to take action and walk the walk.

In order that there is no confusion about whether you are acting with courage or in a courageous way, take a look at Webster's dictionary definition of courage:

Definition of Courage

Courage: mental or moral strength to venture, persevere, and withstand danger, fear, or difficulty; *rage* implies firmness of mind and will in the face of danger or extreme difficulty; *mettle* suggests an ingrained capacity for meeting strain or difficulty with fortitude and resilience; *spirit* also suggests a quality of temperament enabling one to hold one's own or keep up one's morale when opposed or threatened; *resolution* stresses firm determination to achieve one's ends; *tenacity* adds to resolution implications of stubborn persistence and unwillingness to admit defeat.

If you truly wish to succeed in launching your dream career, act with courage. When you take action and take command of your career with courage, you will succeed.

27

Persevere! "Perseverance is a great element of success. If you only knock long enough and loud enough at the gate, you are sure to wake up somebody."
—**Henry Wadsworth Longfellow**

How do you reinvent yourself when one minute you are considered by many to be Superman himself and a split second later you have an accident leaving you unable to walk, talk, and even breathe? Actor Christopher Reeve reinvented himself after a tragic paralyzing horse riding accident in 1995 and persevered against all odds. He persevered in the face of even death itself in order to succeed in launching his own personal reinvention. The following letter to Christopher Reeve exemplifies the honored and respected role perseverance plays in each of our successes.

Dear Mr. Reeve,

Your life has brought new spirit to so many of us who have been inspired by your story. We at the Princeton Montessori School strive to instill the qualities in our children that can carry them throughout their lives, qualities we see in you. Passion, courage, perseverance and self-reliance are the cornerstones of our philosophy. You have been a living example as we have watched you overcome great obstacles in pursuit of your goals.

Since your accident in May 1995, we have watched you transform the entire field of spinal-cord research, continue acting with your roles in The Quest for Camelot *and* Rear Window, *and write your autobiography, among many other more personal achievements.*

We would like to establish this year, on the 30th anniversary of our school, a Christopher Reeve *award. This award, inspired by you, will honor an individual that embodies the values and qualities that you exemplify. Please let us honor you with this award in its inaugural year!*

Source: Princeton Montessori School, December 7, 1998

Like Reeve, with a fraction of the obstacles, you need to persevere with the plans you wrote for yourself in chapter 5. Here is a wonderful story that has inspired me for many years. It is taken from Frank Boreham's *Mushrooms on the Moor.* I hope it will inspire you to persevere with your Career ReExplosion.

A man dwelt in a very comfortable house, with a large, light, airy cellar. The river ran near by. One day the river overflowed, the cellar was flooded, and all the hens that he kept in it were drowned. The next day he bounced off to see the landlord. "I have come," he said, "to give you notice. I wish to leave the house."

"How is that?" asked the astonished landlord. "I thought you liked it so much. It is a very comfortable, well built house, and cheap."

"Oh, yes," the tenant replied, "but the river has overflowed into my cellar, and all my hens are drowned."

"Oh, don't let that make you give up the house," the landlord reasoned; "try ducks!"

28

Go down every path.

Carol Parsons began exploring every possible path for making a career change upon finding herself in a less than ideal situation—a job description that had changed as a result of new management. Parsons states, "I wasn't able to continue doing what I did best, and there was little job satisfaction for me in the way the new management wanted things done. My heart wasn't in it anymore, and I was having a harder and harder time motivating myself, which was always an essential ingredient in my success. So it wasn't a prestige and money issue but more a quality of life issue. All I've ever really wanted out of a career was not to dread going to work in the morning!"

Parsons admits, "I'm not known for my willingness to embrace change." But after eleven successful years in sales, the time had come when she needed to make a change. For Parsons, it did not come easily. It arrived serendipitously after going down a lot of different roads both mentally and physically. "For me, it was quite a long process of moving from the status quo to the utterly unknown. I sent out a lot of résumés and endured no replies. It was a time punctuated with a very great range of highs and lows, determination and frustration, loyalty and disillusionment." In spite of all the frustration and rejection, Parsons persevered. One morning she spoke with a client over breakfast about the usual business issues. To her surprise, the conversation shifted to her desire for a career change. The client then spoke the magic words: "Talk to me." After going down a lot of paths, she had found her new career connection. She was in her new career not many days after that serendipitous path she was willing to go down. Here are Carol Parsons's tips for taking the new career plunge.

- Be patient. Allow transition time.

- Network and ask questions, even if you fear they'll make you look uninformed.

- Be highly organized and efficient.

- Find a mentor. Seek out someone you feel a kindred spirit with and state your intention to come to them for advice occasionally. They'll almost always be flattered and want to help you.

- Remember your strengths! They got you this far. They will see you through this time of career change.

The idea of going down and exploring every path appears to the untrained eye to be an unproductive activity. Therefore, most view the process as negative. For instance, hitting a dead end on a path could be construed as failure both by yourself and your family. That begins a domino effect. Failure breeds "I told you so" from possibly your spouse or a parent. Failure also erodes self-esteem and the desire to persevere. The very process necessary to succeed is avoided by many because of the potentially negative psychological impact. It's like being caught in an undertow. Instead of traveling with it and swimming parallel to the shore, the natural reaction is to expend energy, swim against the undertow, and drown in the process. What seems logical in actuality kills.

29

Revitalize your energy.

To detonate your Career ReExplosion, you are going to need energy, and lots of it. There are two types of energy you will need: mental and physical. Let's talk about the mental energy first and how you are going to get it.

In my previous books I share a lot about self-talk. Self-talk is the internal chatter you speak to yourself at a rate of one thousand words per minute. Have you ever driven home from work and don't remember the last three red lights? Worse yet, when did you not remember the entire drive? Have you ever driven right by the exit to your home off the interstate? All of these are examples of when you were engaged in self-talk. What you speak to yourself is what you get. If it is negative, you are creating negative energy. If it is positive, you are creating positive energy. You can learn more about this powerful energy supply at http://www.selftalk.com.

Along with positive self-talk revitalizing your energy also comes surrounding yourself with positive, like-minded, enthusiastic, and energetic people. Find people who are growing and evolving. Avoid people who have a "been there, done that" attitude. Complete the following Surround Yourself with Positive People Exercise in order to identify people who are going to help give you positive, psychological energy.

SURROUND YOURSELF WITH POSITIVE PEOPLE EXERCISE

Instructions: In the following exercise, there are three columns. In the first, write down the names of all individuals who you learn from and who have a positive influence upon your life. In the second column list all individuals who have a negative and destructive influence upon your life. In the last column list all individuals who have neither a positive nor negative influence. They are neutral. To protect the names of the guilty, you may want to do this exercise on a separate sheet of paper and destroy it when you have the final results. You will receive further instructions at the end of the exercise.

Positive Influence	Negative Influence	Neutral
1. _____	_____	_____
2. _____	_____	_____
3. _____	_____	_____
4. _____	_____	_____
5. _____	_____	_____
6. _____	_____	_____
7. _____	_____	_____

8.		
9.		
10.		

Now that you are finished, go back through the three columns and place a line through all the names in columns two and three. The first column represents the people who are an enormous source of positive energy and inspiration in your life. You can revitalize your energy by spending more time with those who you have listed in the first column. Make a commitment to network and meet more people this month who can be added to this important list. Curtail and at all costs cut off your time with those listed in columns two and three.

The second source of energy that you need to revitalize is your physical energy. Review the guidelines for longevity outlined in chapter 2. We've all heard the most recent research on health, energy, and fitness. Here is a quick review based on current public awareness. There is nothing much more to be said other than to just do it.

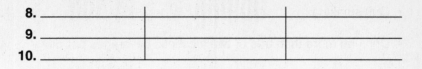

HEALTH, ENERGY, AND FITNESS REVIEW

• Walk, run, swim, inline skate, or engage in another aerobic exercise for thirty minutes three to four times a week.

• Avoid fatty foods.

• Eat lots of grains, fruits, vegetables, and complex carbohydrates.

- Quit smoking.

- Drink no more than one or two alcoholic beverages per day.

- Control your intake of desserts and other sources of processed sugars.

- Keep cholesterol and triglycerides within target limits.

- Keep blood pressure within target limits.

- Stay within 5 percent of your ideal body weight.

- Get adequate amounts of sleep.

- Maintain a maximum body fat content of 18 percent.

- Limit caffeine to the equivalent of two cups of coffee per day.

Physically and mentally take the time to revitalize your energy. Make a new commitment now to maintain positive self-talk and disciplined exercise and eating habits. Detonating your successful Career ReExplosion depends on your ability to maintain an enormous energy supply.

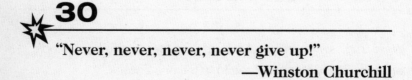

30

"Never, never, never, never give up!"
—Winston Churchill

In Bloomington, Indiana, the first and second grade classes have a few elementary lessons for adults about the importance of never giving up. First, the second grade class has created a list of people who they admire because they achieved their goals despite difficulties. Are you ready to take coaching from a bunch of kids?

BRITTANY, DELVAL, AND CALBY FROM MRS. ELDER'S SECOND GRADE CLASS LIST OF PEOPLE WHO CONTINUED DESPITE DIFFICULTIES

Martin Luther King	Pilgrims	Abraham Lincoln
Laura Ingalls Wilder	Poon Lim	George Washington
Michael Jordan	John Glenn	Columbus
Gandhi	Marie Curie	Moses
Joseph (Bible)	Noah (Bible)	Ralph Nader
Jesus	Me!	My great-grandma
Mom	Dad	Mount Everest climbers

Not to be outdone, the first grade class has something to say about never giving up as well. They share some quotes from people they have studied in school who they discovered have led by example and who never gave up. Next are some actual testimonials of students from the class who we can learn from. They are children who went out and never gave up.

MRS. NELSON'S FIRST GRADE CLASS QUOTES FROM PEOPLE WHO NEVER GAVE UP

- "You're never a loser until you quit trying." —Mike Ditka

- "Mistakes are the doorway to discovery." —Sam Horn

GARY JOSEPH GRAPPO

- "If you've never failed, it's probably because you never tried anything very difficult." —Clint Nelson

- "Never, never, never, never give up!" —Winston Churchill

TESTIMONIALS FROM MRS. NELSON'S FIRST GRADE CLASS

- "One time I was playing basketball with my dad and I couldn't shoot it. I kept trying and I made two baskets." —Allison

- "When I was writing a letter, I didn't know a hard word. I kept trying and I figured it out." —Kyle

- "In Florida I was climbing a rock. It was really big. I kept trying and I got to the top." —Makinzey

A final footnote of inspiration: Mrs. Nelson's class likes the story *The Little Engine That Could*. The engine said, "I think I can, I think I can!"

Adults have a real problem with never giving up. Adults are often more concerned about what others think of them than succeeding. Children, because they know they are in a learning situation in life, are more apt to try new things and not worry about failure. In reality, adults need to realize that with childlike faith, success is usually just on the other side of failure. Many adults never realize success because they are unwilling to work beyond the point of failure. In this section, I took the approach of children teaching adults about never giving up because adults make it too complex. It's very simple. You made a commitment to go out and create your dream careers. It's not going to be easy. Take it from a bunch of kids. You can do it. Just never give up!

TIPS TO HAVE AN ADULT ATTITUDE ABOUT NEVER GIVING UP

- Reassess failure. If you're not failing, you're not doing anything.

- Adversity makes you stronger.

- Failure builds character.

- If you were always on the mountaintop, how would you get food from the valley?

- The more you fail, the closer you are to success.

- Thomas Edison had nearly ten thousand failures before inventing the lightbulb.

- Educate family and friends about your failures as mere steps to success.

- If you fail at the same thing more than three times, you're not learning.

- Rejoice when you have challenges.

- See challenge as an opportunity to shine.

- Feel the fear, and do it anyway.

- Leap first and look later.

Chapter Review

26. Take action with courage.

27. Persevere! "Perseverance is a great element of success. If you only knock long enough and loud enough at the gate, you are sure to wake up somebody." —Henry Wadsworth Longfellow

28. Go down every path.

29. Revitalize your energy.

30. "Never, never, never, never give up!" —Winston Churchill

Career ReExplosion Activity Planner

WHY are some people with high IQs considered unsuccessful, while others with seemingly lower IQs are extremely successful? According to Brian Tracy, the author of *The Science of Self-Confidence* audio series, IQ has nothing to do with success. Tracy believes success is related to the number of actions that an individual is willing to take in his or her life. He states, "No matter how smart you are, if you act stupidly, then you are stupid. Being successful has nothing to do with intelligence. If you act intelligently, then you are intelligent."

Because success is determined by taking action and not necessarily by intelligence alone, this book comes with an action-oriented Activity Planner. It is not enough to talk a good game or to just have good ideas. If that's all life is—discussions, ideas, and theories—then getting to the next stage is never going to happen. Taking actions with calculated risks and wise choices along the way will definitely get you anywhere you want to go.

The Activity Planner is what makes my system, now a series of books, In Thirty Days, effective. It is the only book and series of its kind that monitor key and critical success activities on a daily basis. This book and the Activity Planner are practically the only tools you will ever need to detonate your own Career ReExplosion.

The Activity Planner also provides you with a concise synopsis of the thirty key concepts laid out in this book's success system. As you participate daily in the Activity Planner, you will notice that each day features a corresponding key concept that you learned earlier in the book. You won't have to sift through pages of information to remember the key points.

This action plan provides you with two attack options. The first is to work diligently at the dream career plans that you created in chapter 5, five days a week for thirty days. The second is to work nonstop at your Career ReExplosion plans seven days a week for thirty days. Deciding to work on your plan five days a week provides you at the end of thirty days with forty new business contacts to help fuel your new career explosion. However, for those of you with the time, to assure even greater success, I recommend pursuing the thirty-day-straight option. Here, you receive a total of sixty contacts. Should you decide on this option, fill in the pages marked Bonus Days, to represent weekends. The difference between forty and sixty could mean having or not having achieved your goal rapidly. Commit yourself to the extra work for thirty days if you can afford the time. I don't recommend doing it much longer than that for obvious health and family reasons. But, if you put in the extra effort, it will get your dream careers off and running quickly and successfully.

This action plan also requires using your computer and the Internet on a frequent basis. To remain on the cutting edge and ahead of the competition, you need to commit to becoming completely technologically literate if your aren't already. For instance, this plan requires that you take the time to use E-mail to send follow-up messages to your key contacts. By using your computer and accessing the Internet, you will be able to research your dream careers and remain informed about them on a daily basis. You will even be able to use your computer and the Internet to generate leads and to network. There is a section in the Activity Planner to help you do that.

The Internet activities are required activities in order to diversify and maximize the effective launch of your dream careers. As soon as possible, make the additional investment to create your very own site on the Internet. Get the right advice. However important these Internet activities are, they do not replace the day-to-day conventional activities outlined in this plan.

Be aware that day one represents a Monday. Begin your action plan on a Monday, when you are fresh and a new business week has begun. Also, it will keep in line the bonus days as weekends, should you decide to increase the quantity and quality of your success.

The Activity Planner is a step-by-step action plan that, when diligently followed, will detonate your own Career ReExplosion. Follow closely the steps listed here, and fully complete the Activity Planner. The Activity Planner must be completed on a daily basis to assure that you are putting the proper amount of work and strategy into your dream career plans. Remember, do not rely on good luck. Rely on a good plan—the Activity Planner.

The Activity Planner

BELIEF CHECK

Today I believe I will achieve my Career ReExplosion goal! (Check one.)

_____ I believe all day long. I have no doubts whatsoever.

_____ Okay, I have my doubts, but I'm still focused on my goals.

_____ I have almost given up. I may not make it.

GOAL CHECK

Today I have rededicated my time, energy, and resources to pursuing three possible dream careers. They are listed below. (Refine daily as needed.)

Dream Careers

1. _____

2. _____

3. _____

CHECK SELF-PROMOTION

Today I told at least two new contacts who are listed below about my Career ReExplosion goals and dream career plans.

Name	Company Name	Address	Phone
1. _____	_____	_____	_____
2. _____	_____	_____	_____

CHECK ACTION PLANS

Today I took the following specific actions from the plans I created in chapter 5 and acted upon them. They are listed below.

Today's Actions

1. _____

2. _____

3. _____

CHECK FOLLOW-UP PHONE CALLS
AND THANK YOU NOTES

Today I followed up with at least two previous contacts who are listed below who are helping me with my Career ReExplosion goals and dream career plans. I called or sent them a thank you note.

Name   **Company Name**

1. _____

2. _____

CHECK FOLLOW-UP E-MAIL

Today I utilized E-mail to follow up with at least three key contacts.

Name   **Company Name**

1. _____

2. _____

3. _____

CHECK INTERNET RESEARCH

Today I researched on the Internet sites related to my Career ReExplosion plans and learned of at least three that can help me with my dream career plans.

Site Name	Address	Notes
1.		
2.		
3.		

CHECK MENTORS AND ROLE MODELS

I am developing mentoring and role-model relationships with the following individuals. (Add and change as necessary.)

Name	Address	Phone
1.		
2.		
3.		

✴ Week 1

DAY 1

Remember your childhood dreams. Recall the things that interested you as a child.

DAY 2

Identify your current dreams. What passions, skills, and interests have you acquired as an adult?

DAY 3

Diversify! Choose three Career ReExplosion options that will make you happy.

DAY 4

In your disbelief, believe you can do it.

DAY 5

Surround yourself with family and friends who will believe with you.

BONUS DAY 6

Eliminate friends who do not support your Career ReExplosion aspirations.

BONUS DAY 7

Rekindle your childhood curiosity for trying new things.

✹ Week 2

DAY 8
Be creative and unconventional.

DAY 9
Identify transferable skills.

DAY 10
Build relationships with mentors and role models.

DAY 11
Do your research.

DAY 12
Join or form a support group.

BONUS DAY 13
Volunteer.

BONUS DAY 14
Acquire the right credentials.

Week 3

DAY 15

Take personal responsibility.

DAY 16

Write a Career ReExplosion plan and divide it into small, active steps.

DAY 17

Divide the plan into two chapters: actions for the immediate present and actions for the immediate future.

DAY 18

Write a one-page introduction to each plan, identifying your vision and mission for your dream career.

DAY 19

Be flexible and let your plan evolve. The shortest route to where you are going will not always be a straight line.

BONUS DAY 20

"Never let the fear of striking out get in your way." —Babe Ruth

BONUS DAY 21

Implement the new you beginning right now.

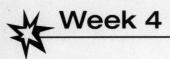

Week 4

DAY 22

Restructure your time and priorities.

DAY 23

Ask for the help of others and get them involved.

DAY 24

Promote yourself.

DAY 25

What you speak is what you get.

DAY 26

Take action with courage.

BONUS DAY 27

Persevere! "Perseverance is a great element of success. If you only knock long enough and loud enough at the gate, you are sure to wake up somebody." —Henry Wadsworth Longfellow

BONUS DAY 28

Go down every path.

Week 5

DAY 29

Revitalize your energy.

DAY 30

"Never, never, never, never give up!" —Winston Churchill

Bibliography

Alea, Pat, and Mullins, Patty. *The Best Work of Your Life.* New York, NY: Penguin Putnam Inc., 1998.

Armour, Stephanie. "Boredom Drains Workers, Workforce," *USA Today.* May 21, 1999, p. 12, section B.

Augustine, Rosemary. Career Advice. http://www.careeradvice.com

Barrett, Jim, and Williams, Geoff. *Test Your Own Job Aptitude.* New York, NY: Penguin, 1992.

Boreham, Frank. *Mushrooms on the Moor.* London: The Epworth Press, 1930, p. 52–53.

Chandler, Steve. *ReInventing Yourself.* New York: Career Press, 1998.

Drucker, Peter. *Management Challenges for the 21st Century.* New York: Harper Business, 1999.

Eikelberry, Carol. *The Career Guide for Creative and Unconventional People.* Berkeley, CA: Ten Speed Press, 1995.

Foisy, Michel. *The Law of Personal Responsibility.* http://www.connectmmic.net/users/foisy

Gawain, Shakti. *Creative Visualization*. New York: Bantam Books, 1995.

Goleman, Daniel. *Emotional Intelligence*. New York: Bantam Books, 1995.

Grappo, Gary Joseph. *Get the Job You Want in Thirty Days*. New York: Berkley, 1997.

———. *Start Your Own Business in Thirty Days*. New York: Berkley, 1998.

———. *The Top 10 Fears of Job Seekers*. New York: Berkley Books, 1996.

———. *The Top 10 Career Strategies for Making a Living in the Year 2000 and Beyond*. New York: Berkley, 1997.

Hekimi, Siegfried, and Lakowski, Bernard. "A Central Physiological Clock in *C. elegans*," *Science*. May 17, 1996.

Lakowski. "Determination of life-span in *Caenorhabditis elegans* by Four Clock Genes," *Science*, 272:1010–1013, 1996.

Lancaster, Hal. "A Sales Executive Makes a Bold Leap," *The Wall Street Journal*, April 27, 1999.

Landes, Michael. *The 1998 Back Door Guidebook*. Chico, CA: Back Door Experiences, 1998.

McGinn, Daniel, and McCormick, John. "Your Next Job," *Newsweek*, Feb. 1, 1999: 43–51.

Potter, Beverly. *Overcoming Job Burnout*. New York: Ronin Publishing, 1998.

Rosen, Stephen, and Paul, Celia. *Career Renewal*. San Diego, CA: Academic Press, 1998.

Ross, M., and Fletcher, G.J.O. "Attribution and Social Perception." In: *The Handbook of Social Psychology*. 3rd Ed., 2 vols. (eds.) Gardner Lindzey and Eliot Aranson. New York: Random House, 1985.

Schwartz, Joyce A. *Successful Recareering*. Hawthorne, NJ: Career Press, 1993.

Sheehy, Gail. *New Passages*. New York: Random House, 1995.

Spragins, Ellyn E. "How to Beat Job Lock," *Newsweek*, Dec. 14, 1998: 98.

Sullivan, H. S. *The Interpersonal Theory of Psychiatry*. New York: W. W. Norton and Co., 1972.

Teich, Albert H., *Technology and the Future*, New York: St. Martins, 1996.

Thompson, C. "Concepts of Self in the Interpersonal Theory," *American Journal of Psychotherapy*, 12:5–17, 1958.

Tracy, Brian, *The Science of Self-Confidence* (tape series). Solana Beach, CA: Brian Tracy, 1990.

Contact the Author Directly

Gary Grappo is considered to be one of the most successful and prolific authors and business/career coaches in the world today. His books are published worldwide from Tokyo and London to Taiwan and New York. For more information about how you, your company, or organization could best utilize Gary Grappo's expert coaching as listed below, please contact him at ASTEC International Human Asset Technologies, Inc. Call for more information at (954) 484-6495. Correspond with him on the Internet at ggrappo@mindspring.com. The Internet address for Gary Grappo is http://www.CareerEdgeOnline.com.

• **Corporate Training and Development:** Developing people with important life skills such as customer service, sales, telemarketing, management development, time management, team building, senior executive coaching, and more.

- **Grappo's Career Success Strategies:** Talks and coaching concerning important topics such as image, attitude, entrepreneurism, intrapreneurism, self-marketing, résumés, cover letters, career testing, personality assessments, and more.

- **Millennium Career Tactics:** Prepare now to remain employed in the future with topics such as Old Game—New Rules, The Future Growth Industries/Regions, Managing Change, Going Global, Techno Literacy Expectations, Emotional Intelligence in the Workplace, and more.

- **Career ReExplosion:** Whether your organization is a group of seniors emerging out of retirement or seniors in high school entering the workforce, you'll want Mr. Grappo to come and cover the following topics: How to Identify a Dream Career, Dream Skill Personal Assessments, How to Take Courage and Take Action, Wake up, Quit Your Old Job and Move On!, and more.

- **In Thirty Days:** How to master and change almost any aspect of your life and career in thirty days. Talks are constructed and tailored for your group directly from Mr. Grappo's *In Thirty Days* book series.

Note: All seminars, talks, and coaching come complete with a complimentary book for all participants.